SCRIBES, SCROLLS, AND SCRIPTURE

Authors in the Biblical Classics Library:

C.K. Barrett
  The Signs of an Apostle (19)
F.F. Bruce
  Men and Movements in the Primitive Church (13)
  The Message of the New Testament (1)
  The Pauline Circle (14)
David Burnett
  The Healing of the Nations (18)
D.A. Carson
  From Triumphalism to Maturity (20)
  Jesus and His Friends (15)
  The Sermon on the Mount (2)
  When Jesus Confronts the World (16)
H.L. Ellison
  Men Spake from God (9)
  The Message of the Old Testament (3)
John Goldingay
  God's Prophet, God's Servant (5)
Graeme Goldsworthy
  Gospel and Kingdom (4)
  Gospel and Wisdom (10)
  The Gospel in Revelation (6)
J.H. Greenlee
  Scribes, Scrolls and Scripture (17)
R.T. Kendall
  Believing God (11)
  Jonah (12)
I. Howard Marshall
  The Work of Christ (7)
Leon Morris
  The Cross of Jesus (8)
A.W. Wolters
  Creation Regained (21)

Scribes, Scrolls, and Scripture

J. HAROLD GREENLEE

paternoster press

Copyright © Wm. B. Eerdmans Publishing Co. 1985

First published in the U.K. 1996
by Paternoster Press, P.O. Box 300, Carlisle, Cumbria CA3 0QS
in the Biblical Classics Library
by arrangement with Wm. B. Eerdmans Publishing Co.,
255 Jefferson Ave. S.E., Grand Rapids, MI 49503, U.S.A.

02 01 00 99 98 97 96   7 6 5 4 3 2 1

British Library Cataloguing in Publication Data

A catalogue record for this book is available from the British Library.

ISBN 0–85364–741–0

Printed in the U.K. by Cox & Wyman Ltd., Reading

Contents

To
Ruth
Dorothy   Lois   David

Preface

Today, as in the past, the average Christian who loves and reads his New Testament is sadly uninformed about the background and history of this most important book. He tends to think of it as an English book. He also tends to think of it as speaking a special form of English; many Christians still feel a bit uneasy about a Bible that does not sound a bit ancient. Indeed, the King James Version of the Bible, surely one of the masterpieces of English literature, was the Bible for English readers for so many generations that this translation is often regarded as the "real" Bible, to which any other version should be compared for approval.

Yet the New Testament is a Greek book—or rather a collection of books—written by several authors under the inspiration of the Holy Spirit nineteen hundred years ago, and written in the kind of Greek that ordinary people spoke every day. Well over a thousand years passed before it was translated into English; it had been translated into many other languages before John Wycliffe first put it into the language of the British peasant. Several subsequent English translations were made before the version authorized by King James of England was published less than four hundred years ago.

Of course, the most important thing is to believe and obey the New Testament, not merely to know the story of its origin. Yet this lack of acquaintance with the history of the New Testament as we have it today has led to misunderstanding and confusion. Some voices are proclaiming that many or all of the recent English translations of the New Testament are corrupted, or are translated from corrupted and heretical ancient manuscripts, and that the King James Version and the Greek manuscripts from which it was translated are the only pure and reliable forms of the New Testament.

How were the books of the New Testament originally written? Can we be sure that the true text of the New Testament has survived in any form after all these centuries? What must we think about the multitude of differences between the ancient manuscripts? Did some ancient scribes intentionally "water down" or corrupt the New Testament text as they were copying it? These are questions that should be of concern to the sincere Christian; these are some of the questions this book attempts to answer in layman's language but with scholarly accuracy.

It is my hope and prayer that this little volume will bring illumination to many people concerning God's word to man, and encouragement to believe that we do have the Word of God in the versions of the New Testament we read today.

CHAPTER ONE

What Ancient Books Looked Like

What did a book of the New Testament look like when it was first written in the year A.D. 50, 60, 70, or some other date in the first Christian century? After the books were written, how were they copied and handed down through the centuries to reach us as we know them now? When we read our New Testament today, can we be sure that we are reading what Luke, John, Paul, and the other authors wrote so long ago? Why do various translations differ with one another? What about the footnotes that say "Other ancient MSS read..."?

These are some of the questions that are answered in the study called "textual criticism."

From the most ancient times until just over five hundred years ago, when someone wrote a book, a poem, a letter, or anything else, there was no way of duplicating it except by hand, one copy at a time. Of course, most of the things that were written—letters, receipts, notices, and such—did not need to be copied. Among the other ancient writings, however, were great pieces of literature of which many people wanted copies, not only soon after they were written but for many centuries afterward. This was the situation with the Bible, too, of course. As a result of this demand, hundreds of ancient manuscripts (i.e., handwritten copies) not only of the

1

biblical books but also of many of the books of other authors of ancient times can be seen today in libraries in many parts of the world. After an author wrote his book (the original manuscript was called an "autograph," meaning "self-writing"), his manuscript was copied, then copies were made from this copy, others from these, and so on, often through several centuries. The autographs of these ancient books, including the Bible, perished ages ago, and we have only copies of copies, most of them many copies away from the originals and therefore differing from the original and from one another to some extent.

It is because of this that the science of textual criticism is needed, for study not only of the Bible but of any ancient writing the original of which is lost. Textual criticism is the study of copies of an ancient writing to try to determine the exact words of the text as the author originally wrote them. Scholars use textual criticism to study the manuscripts of the classical authors, especially the Greek and Latin writers, such as Plato, Herodotus, Homer, Livy, Cicero, and Virgil. Since the Bible is the most important of ancient writings, textual criticism of the Bible, and especially of the New Testament, is the most important field of textual criticism. In this volume we will be concentrating on textual criticism of the New Testament.

It is important to note at the outset, however, that *textual criticism* is not at all the same thing as *literary criticism*, which is sometimes called "higher criticism." Literary criticism attempts to find out the sources underlying an author's work—that is, it tries to determine where he got his information. This "higher criticism" has often been applied to the Bible in a destructive way, and it has come to be looked down on by many evangelical Christians. But as I say, textual criticism is quite distinct from literary criticism. Textual criticism simply takes the known manuscripts of the New Testament, studies the differences between them, and attempts by established principles to determine the exact wording of the New Testament originals.

The Importance of New Testament Textual Criticism

As I just noted, the most important field of textual criticism is the study of the manuscripts of the New Testament. This is true for three reasons. In the first place, the New Testament is the most important of all ancient literary works. In the second place, the number of ancient manuscripts of the New Testament known today is far greater than that of any other ancient book. This gives the New Testament a far greater field for the application of textual criticism. The ancient Greek and Latin classics are known today, in some cases, from only one surviving manuscript. In other cases there are three, fifty, or a hundred manuscripts; at most there are a few hundred. For the New Testament, on the other hand, we presently know of almost five thousand Greek manuscripts, eight thousand Latin manuscripts, and an additional thousand manuscripts in other ancient languages.

In the third place, the manuscripts of the New Testament that are known today include some that were copied much nearer to the time when these books were originally written than is the case with other ancient books. The oldest known manuscripts of some of the Greek classics were copied over a thousand years after the author wrote his book. The oldest known manuscripts of most of the Latin classics were copied from three hundred to seven hundred years after these books were originally written. In the case of the New Testament, however, one manuscript known today that contains most of the Gospel of John was copied less than one hundred years after the Gospel was originally written, and we have numerous manuscripts of various parts of the New Testament that were copied three hundred years or less after the books were originally written.

What can we conclude from all this? Scholars believe that the manuscripts of the ancient classics at their disposal are reliable copies of these ancient books. How much more certain may we be, then, that the manuscripts of the New Testament that we possess give us the original text of the New Testament accurately, since there are so many more of these manuscripts, and since they were copied much nearer the dates when the originals were written!

We should also mention that manuscripts of the New Testament differ greatly in the amount of text they contain. One of the two oldest is a tiny fragment that contains only part of three or four verses of the Gospel of John. Other manuscripts contain the entire New Testament. Between these extremes, various manuscripts contain one New Testament book, one leaf, part of one book, or several books.

Although the many manuscripts of the New Testament differ from one another, we must not exaggerate the importance of the differences that are found in them. There is no question of separating "orthodox" manuscripts from "heretical" ones. In fact, all of the ancient manuscripts contain the Word of God, and they all agree in most of the words of their text. Textual criticism, therefore, deals mostly with small details of differences between the manuscripts.

Why Textual Criticism Is Needed

Perhaps we should speak a bit more specifically about why it is so important to study and compare the ancient manuscripts of the New Testament or of any other ancient book. As we have noted, in ancient times the only way to reproduce a book was to make one copy at a time by hand. This meant not only that copies of the New Testament were expensive but also that no two copies of a New Testament book would be completely identical. Small errors and differences would almost certainly creep in as a result of ordinary human frailty, differences in handwriting, and the fact that the Greek text was written without any breaks between words. When scribes made further copies of these copies, they might discover and correct some errors, but they would unwittingly reproduce most of the errors and add a few more of their own.

Thus, in general, the more copies by which a manuscript is removed from its original the more it may differ from the original. At the same time, it must be emphasized once again that the total of these differences and errors affects only a small portion of the text, especially so far as differences of meaning are concerned. No truth or doctrine of Scripture is placed in doubt by differences between the manuscripts. Yet the New Testament is of such supreme importance that it is well worth our while to study the manuscripts to make even small improvements in our knowledge and our assurance concerning the original words of the authors.

CHAPTER TWO

How Ancient Manuscripts Were Written

Down through the centuries, people have written on a great variety of materials. In ancient times these materials have included such diverse surfaces as the leaves and bark of trees, linen cloth, broken pieces of pottery (called "ostraca" or "potsherds"), walls of buildings, metal, and wooden tablets coated with wax.

Waxed tablet

Waxed Tablets. Waxed tablets were used by people of Greece and Rome before the Christian era. To make these tablets, a piece of wood was hollowed slightly and coated with wax, making something that looked a bit like a child's slate of more recent times. Writing was done with a pointed stick called a stylus, and the writing could be erased by smoothing the wax surface. These tablets were used for temporary writings and for personal correspondence. They were also used at times for legal documents, in which case two tablets would be placed face to face with the writing inside and fastened together with leather thongs run through holes at the edges of the tablets. In one of his writings St. Augustine mentions some tablets he owned, although his were made of ivory instead of wood. Luke 1:63 tells us that Zechariah, the father of John the Baptist, used a tablet, probably of this type (this is what is meant by the phrase "writing table" in the KJV), to write his son's name.

Papyrus. Of course waxed tablets were not suitable for long stories or for any other text that was meant to be read again and again. For literary works the ancient authors used papyrus, the material from which our word *paper* is derived. The oldest known papyrus fragment comes from Egypt and is said to have been written about 2400 B.C. It was the most common writing material in Greece in the fifth century B.C. It was inexpensive and convenient and was used for literary works as well as for such things as letters, receipts, and business matters.

Papyrus plant

The papyrus plant is a reed that grew in swampy areas in the Nile River delta and a few other places in the Mediterranean world. (I personally first saw papyrus plants growing in San José, Costa Rica.) The plant had a triangular stalk (although I am told that those in the Los Angeles Arboretum have round stalks) with a tassel at the top, and grew to a height of six to twelve feet. In order to make writing material, the outer skin of the stalk was stripped off and the pithy center was cut into thin strips. The strips were laid side by side to the desired size and then another layer was laid crosswise on top. Either paste or the juice of the plant may have been used to hold the layers together. Once assembled, the sheets were pounded, dried, and then smoothed with a piece of ivory or a shell.

Papyrus manuscript construction: One layer of strips was pasted crosswise over another layer

The pith of the papyrus plant was called *biblos*, from which such English words as "bibliography" and "Bible" are derived. A papyrus sheet is mentioned in 2 John 12. The Greek word in this verse (*chartes*, from which the English word "chart" is derived) is translated "paper" in various English versions.

Papyrus sheets were made in sizes from about six by nine inches to twelve by fifteen inches. The sheets were overlapped slightly and pasted together in long strips of twenty sheets, then rolled up for sale. Of course, the purchaser could paste several rolls together if he wanted to produce a long text. Some New Testament books, for example, would require several rolls. The Gospel of Matthew would make a roll nearly thirty feet long, which was about the practical limit for the length of a papyrus scroll.

During the time of the Roman Empire the government controlled the papyrus trade. As the rolls were prepared for sale, the names of the officials responsible for this trade would be written on the first page. The Greek term for this first page was *protokollon*, or "first glued sheet," and it is this word that has given us our English word "protocol."

A book written on these papyrus rolls was called a *biblos* or *biblion*. This word appears several times in the New Testament, including Matthew 1:1, Luke 3:4, and Acts 1:20. It means "scroll" rather than "book" as we think of the term. If a book required several scrolls, each scroll or volume was called a *tomos*, which means "cutting." Even in our day a large, scholarly book is sometimes called a "weighty tome."

Scroll

Writing was done on the side of the scroll on which the papyrus strips were laid horizontally, and the scroll was always rolled so that this would be the inside of the scroll. It was more difficult to write on the other side of the scroll, where the papyrus strips were laid vertically, because this entailed writing across the fibers of the papyrus. Only rarely was this done; however, Revelation 5:1 refers to such a scroll written on both sides, probably to indicate that the author had so much to say that he could not get it all written on the proper side of the scroll.

The Egyptians exported papyrus rolls to other countries. Papyrus was the most common writing material until the third Christian century, and it continued to be used for secular classical literature until the sixth or seventh century. So it is clear that the original manuscripts of the New Testament were written on papyrus. Papyrus sheets were perishable, however, and few books or other documents written on papyrus in ancient times have survived except in a few very dry places, such as the sands of Egypt.

Parchment. The skins of animals, made into scrolls of tanned leather, were also used to receive writing in ancient times. Skins made strong and durable rolls. They were used by the Persians, the Greeks, and especially by the Hebrews, but not much by the Egyptians, since Egypt had a plentiful supply of papyrus. The oldest leather scroll presently known is one written in 1468 B.C. describing the victory by King Tuthmosis III at Megiddo in that year. The Hebrews continued to use leather scrolls for their scriptures long into the Christian era, and even now leather scrolls of the Hebrew Old Testament are common in Jewish places of worship.

It was a later improvement, however, that brought animal skins into common use as a writing material. In this process, instead of being tanned, the skins were soaked in quicklime water and the hair was scraped off. The skins were scraped on both sides, dried, and rubbed with chalk and pumice stone. The result was a fine, smooth writing surface of long-lasting quality.

Skins treated in this way were known as "vellum" or "parchment." *Vellum* properly means "calfskin" (the word veal is related to it), but the term was later applied to other skins of finer quality as well. The word "parchment" comes from the name of the city Pergamus, which was noted for the quality of parchment produced there. The term was originally used to denote skins of lesser quality than the finer vellum. Now, however, the two terms are commonly used interchangeably.

When we compare the writing surfaces of papyrus and parchment, it seems surprising that people at first considered parchment inferior to papyrus. Papyrus continued to be the "proper" material for literary works, while parchment was used for such things as business papers, notebooks, and the first drafts of an author's works. As time passed, however, parchment began to replace papyrus as the accepted material for a "book." This occurred partly because as the need for writing materials increased, the supply of papyrus was not sufficient. The fact that it was easier to write on parchment and the fact that parchment documents lasted much longer likely constituted an even greater influence in effecting the changeover. At any rate, by the fourth century of the Christian era, parchment had displaced papyrus as the most common writing material, although papyrus continued to be used for another three centuries for classical literature and occasionally for New Testament manuscripts.

The very earliest known manuscripts of the New Testament, those that come from the second and third centuries, are on papyrus. During the fourth century, however, scribes began copying the New Testament on parchment, and parchment was the material used for almost all New Testament manuscripts from that time until paper came into use a thousand years later.

Paper. The invention of paper is attributed to a Chinese man named Tsai Lun, in A.D. 89. The oldest existing specimens of Chinese paper, from the fourth century, are made of hemp or flax. Paper became known to the Arabs about the eighth century and was introduced into the Western world at the time of the Crusades. Paper came to be used for books in Europe in the twelfth century and had practically replaced parchment by the fifteenth century. This was a timely development, since the invention of the printing press soon afterward brought about a markedly increased demand for writing material that parchment could not have met.

Implements People Used for Writing

When someone wrote on a waxed tablet, as we have noted, he used a pointed stick, or stylus, much like the stylus that is used today for writing by hand on a mimeograph stencil. The other end of the stylus usually had a rounded knob, which was used for erasing and making corrections.

For writing on papyrus, a pen made from a reed (called a *kalamos* in Greek) was commonly used. It is this sort of pen that is referred to in 3 John 13, which mentions writing "with pen and ink." To make this type of pen, the stalk of a hollow reed was cut and allowed to dry a bit. Then one end was sharpened to a point with a sloping cut, and a slit was made extending up the stem about a quarter inch from the point. Pens of this type were flexible, which

Reed pens

made them suitable for writing on the fibrous surface of papyrus. After being used for a time, the point would become frayed and need to be resharpened. Indeed, the very earliest reed pens now known were evidently made with a frayed end like a small brush; scribes began to use the pointed form about the third century before Christ. Although such a pen might seem to us to be a rather crude instrument, papyrus manuscripts demonstrate that a good scribe could produce beautiful writing with a good reed pen.

Quill pens

A different kind of pen is familiar to most of us from pictures we have seen representing people writing in past centuries—the quill pen. Quill pens came into use later than reed pens. They would have been too firm for satisfactory writing on papyrus, but they were well suited for parchment. The quill pen was formed by sharpening a goose feather to a point, much like a reed pen, but it lasted much longer than the reed pen.

In these days of ballpoint pens, we hardly give a thought to ink as a separate item. However, the older ones among us may remember the days of an ink bottle or an inkwell on the school desk and a pen with a steel point that had to be dipped into the ink after every few words. This is how writing was done with a reed or quill pen. Two kinds of ink were common in ancient times, and both can be seen in the manuscripts that have come down to us. One type of ink was made of lampblack (a substance like the carbon that collects on a dish held over a candle flame) and gum dissolved in water. This type of ink produced black writing. The other type was made from nut galls, and produced a fine rusty brown writing. Red ink was often used for headings and initial letters, and other colors (even purple, gold, and silver) were sometimes used for special manuscripts. *Melas*, the Greek word for "black," is the word used for *ink* in 2 John

12 and 3 John 13, which probably indicates that black ink was the color most commonly used.

The well-equipped scribe's desk would include some other aids as well, such as a knife for making or repairing his pens, a whetstone for sharpening his knife, a bit of pumice stone for smoothing rough spots in his parchment sheets and for sharpening his pen point, and a sponge for erasing and wiping his pen.

"Books" in Ancient Times

The Scroll. The papyrus scroll books of the first century did not have an opening title page as we are accustomed to; rather, the title of the book was usually written at the end of the scroll. However, a papyrus tag containing the title was often attached to the scroll as an aid to the reader.

The columns of writing in a scroll were rather narrow, from two to three inches wide, so that the scroll would not have to be opened wide to be read. Space between the columns of writing was likewise narrow. The writing on a scroll was always done so that the scroll was held and opened horizontally, never vertically (in spite of the pictures so common on Christmas cards and the like, which mistakenly show someone holding a scroll open vertically). The scroll would be unrolled toward the left for Greek and Latin, which are written from left to right, and in the opposite direction for Hebrew, which is written from right to left. In some cases the scroll may have been rolled around a stick or roller (decorated rollers are quite common in Hebrew biblical scrolls), but more often the scroll was simply rolled on itself. When a reader or writer had completed a scroll, he would reroll it by holding it under his chin and rolling it with both hands. It was considered to be a mark of laziness if a reader failed to reroll his book when he had finished with it.

There are obvious disadvantages to a book in scroll form, as anyone who has attempted to locate a particular page in a long microfilm roll will attest. It was difficult to turn quickly to specific columns within a scroll, and if a reader wanted to interrupt his reading, there would be the question of whether he should reroll the scroll and unroll it again later or leave it opened in some safe place. There was even a proverb: "A great book, a great evil."

Papyrus scrolls are mentioned several times in the New Testament; references are usually translated as "book." Luke 4:17 speaks of the scroll (*biblion*) of the prophet Isaiah. John uses the same word to refer to his Gospel in John 20:30. The "books" or "scrolls" mentioned in 2 Timothy 4:13 may be either parchment scrolls or leather scrolls of the Old Testament. Revelation 6:14 describes the sky as vanishing like "a scroll when it is rolled up."

The Codex. Although the scroll was the accepted form for a book in the first Christian century, there are no known surviving ancient manuscripts of the New Testament in scroll form. The early Christians often examined Old Testament passages to relate them to their faith, and looking up widely separated references in a scroll was a time-consuming task. A bit later, when some of the New Testament books had been written, the same problem arose in studying various parts of these books. As a result, when a form of book different from the scroll came into use, Christians were quick to see its advantages and began using this new form for their scriptures when new copies were made. Indeed, scholars credit Christianity with exercising the greatest single influence in bringing about this change of book forms for works of literature.

Codex

The new book form that replaced the scroll is basically the same as the book form we use today. The "codex" (plural *codices*), as it is called, takes its form from the ancient waxed tablets that were fastened together at one side with leather thongs as hinges. A codex was formed by laying several sheets—usually four—one on top of the other, folding them together, and then sewing them at the fold. This made a "quire." Then as many quires as were needed were bound together, as is done in modern books. In a papyrus codex, the sheets would be placed so that at any given opening both pages would have either horizontal or vertical strips. In parchment quires, facing pages would be either the hair side or the flesh side of the skin.

From our idea of a book, it may seem strange that when the codex was first developed it was regarded as a sort of notebook, to be used for letters, business papers, or for the first draft of an author's book or poems, and that the final "published" work would be in a scroll. As time passed, the advantages of the codex for works of literature became evident, however. Christians began to copy their scriptures in codex manuscripts at an early date, although we cannot be sure exactly when. Since the Gospels and Acts were "books," it seems probable that they were initially written by their authors on papyrus scrolls. At the same time, scholars speculate that a problem involving the last twelve verses of Mark that we will investigate in a later chapter could have resulted from the loss of some text from the autograph or a very early copy. It would have been much easier to lose the final page or quire from a codex than to lose the last portion of a scroll, since the last portion of a scroll would normally be at the inside of the roll.

The epistles of the New Testament, on the other hand, with the possible exception of Hebrews, were not written as books but as letters to churches and individuals. These may therefore have been written originally on papyrus codices.

At any rate, even the oldest manuscripts of the New Testament known today do not take us back to a time when it was copied on scrolls. The oldest New Testament manuscript now known, as we mentioned earlier, is a small papyrus fragment in the Rylands Library of Manchester, England, containing about four verses of John's Gospel. It is clearly part of a codex, not a scroll, since the text is written on both sides of the papyrus. Nearly as old is a papyrus codex in the Bodmer Library of Geneva, Switzerland, containing most of John. Both of these manuscripts were copied about A.D. 150. More than thirty other papyrus codices from the second, third, and fourth centuries are known today.

About the middle of the fourth century, scribes began copying on parchment. From that time, the parchment codex was the accepted form for New Testament manuscripts, although a number of papyrus codices from later centuries have come down to us.

In addition to the fact that a codex could be opened quickly at any point, this book form had another distinct advantage. The longest practical length for a scroll was about thirty feet. Using handwriting of ordinary size, a roll of this length could contain no more than· one of the longer books of the New Testament, such as Matthew or Acts. A papyrus codex, on the other hand, could contain much more. Among the manuscripts of the Chester Beatty Library in Dublin, for example, is one papyrus codex that originally contained the four Gospels and Acts, and another that contained the Pauline epistles and Hebrews. With the further change from papyrus to parchment, it became possible to include the entire New Testament in one volume. Indeed, two of the most famous New Testament manuscripts, Codex Vaticanus of the Vatican Library and Codex Sinaiticus of the British Museum, originally contained both the Old and New Testaments.

Since the supply of parchment was not inexhaustible, and the sheets were quite durable, when a parchment codex was no longer wanted, or if some of its pages had become damaged, the manuscript was sometimes taken apart, the damaged leaves were discarded, and the text was scraped off the usable leaves so that the text of a different manuscript could be written on them. A manuscript rewritten in this manner is called a "palimpsest," from two Greek words meaning "to scrape again." Even New Testament manuscripts were erased in this way. Indeed, more than fifty Greek New Testament palimpsests are known. Happily, the standards of erasing were not too high, and much of the text of these erased manuscripts can be read through and between the lines of the later text with patience, good eyes, and sometimes with the help of a magnifying glass or with scientific techniques involving the use of ultraviolet or infrared light.

The Handwriting in the Manuscripts

From before the beginning of the Christian era there were two kinds of Greek handwriting. One type is called "uncial" letters, which are a good deal like English capital letters in style, but rounded off to some extent and adapted for fairly rapid writing, although they were not connected. For many centuries uncial letters were the most common type of handwriting used in manuscripts of literary works, whether on papyrus scrolls, papyrus codices, or parchment codices. The words were written with no spaces between them, not to save space but simply as the accepted custom.

The other form of handwriting, known as "cursive," might be likened to a mixture of English longhand and lower-case printing, although the letters are less connected than they are in English longhand writing. This style of handwriting was used for personal and business writing such as letters and receipts. Cursive writing could be done much more quickly than uncial writing. Paul's letters to Timothy, Titus, and Philemon may have been written in cursive handwriting originally, since these were personal letters.

As time passed, it appears that scribes began to be interested in a more rapid way of copying manuscripts than was possible with uncial letters. Eventually, early in the ninth century, a new style of handwriting was developed. This new form of letters, called "minuscule," meaning "rather small," was a modification of cursive handwriting that was more formal and more legible than ordinary cursive. It was possible to write much more rapidly with minuscule letters than with uncial letters because of the form of the letters and the fact that some letters could be connected. One of the oldest minuscule New Testament manuscripts is a manuscript of the Gospels; it is the oldest known manuscript to contain a date based on the birth of Christ, as are our present calendars: it states that it was written in A.D. 835.

During the following century or so scribes began using the minuscule handwriting more and more in copying manuscripts, and by the end of the tenth century the period of

Codex 048, a palimpsest. The original text is an uncial manuscript dating from the fifth century; this folio includes Acts 28:3-20, written three columns to the page. The later minuscule text, containing writings of St. Gregory Nazianzen, was written in the tenth or eleventh centuries and is shown here upside down. (Used by permission of the Vatican Library.)

Codex 747, a minuscule manuscript written in A.D. 1164. The larger writing, centered on the right, contains the biblical text, Luke 2:1-7. The smaller writing wrapped around it comprises excerpts from the writings of various Church Fathers. (Used by permission of the Bibliotheque Nationale, Paris.)

uncial letters had come to an end. It can easily be remembered, therefore, that uncial manuscripts were produced in the tenth century or earlier, and minuscule manuscripts were produced in the ninth century or later. About ninety percent of the known Greek New Testament manuscripts are minuscules.

Another general clue to the age of a manuscript is the fact that in both the uncial and minuscule periods the earlier manuscripts have little or no ornamentation, whereas the later manuscripts tend to have more decoration (often called "illumination"), in some cases including large ornamented initial letters at the opening of a book or the beginning of a new section.

Various contractions are found in manuscripts. The type that is most interesting is a special group of fifteen words called "sacred names" (the Latin term is *nomina sacra*) that are abbreviated by using the first one or two letters plus the last letter or letters of the word, with a horizontal line over the letters to indicate that it is an abbreviation. This group of words includes "God" ($\overline{\theta\varsigma}$), "Christ" ($\overline{\chi\varsigma}$), "Jerusalem" ($\overline{I\lambda\eta\mu}$), and others.

CHAPTER THREE

The Ancient Records
of the Greek New Testament

e have talked about how the ancient manuscripts were made and copied. We should now investigate these manuscripts as records in which the New Testament has been handed down to us through the centuries. How do we know today what the New Testament writers actually wrote back in the latter part of the first Christian century? What are the kinds of manuscripts in which the Scriptures were preserved until the invention of printing from movable type made it possible to make an unlimited number of identical copies of a book?

Greek Manuscripts

Autographs. The first group of manuscripts we should note is a group we don't have—the autographs, the original manuscripts of the New Testament books. Some authors may have penned their books themselves; others may have dictated to a secretary, or "amanuensis." Some of Paul's letters indicate that he used an amanuensis. Romans 16:22, for example, reads "I Tertius, who wrote this letter, greet you." 2 Thessalonians 3:17 reads "The greeting by the hand of me, Paul, which is the sign in every letter; this is how I write," implying that someone else had written the rest of the letter at his dictation. 1 Corinthians 16:21, Galatians 6:11, and Colossians 4:18 have similar greetings from Paul said to have been produced in his own handwriting.

Papyri. The earliest manuscripts actually known to exist today are papyrus manuscripts in codex form. To date over seventy of these manuscripts have been discovered. Their contents and size vary from the tiny Rylands fragment we have already mentioned to codices that contain large portions of several New Testament books.

The first discovery of papyrus manuscripts in modern times was made in 1778, in the Fayum province of Egypt. More were found from time to time covered with sand or in rubbish heaps, preserved by the dry air of the region. Most of these papyri were nonliterary documents—receipts, personal letters, property deeds, and the like. For almost one hundred years their significance was not realized, and some were burned or destroyed in other ways. It was late in the nineteenth century when scholars began to realize that even these humble writings were actually treasures because of the light their contents shed on customs, ideas, culture, and the language of their times. A book entitled *Light from the Ancient East*, by Adolf Deissmann, gives a great deal of interesting information about these papyri.

A different and very important kind of treasure, however, was also found in these same rubbish heaps: works of ancient literature, both secular classics and biblical manuscripts, including some of the oldest manuscripts yet discovered of these writings.

Papyrus manuscripts of the New Testament have been discovered almost nowhere other than in Egypt.

For the purposes of textual criticism, all New Testament papyri are designated by "P" followed by a number. The Rylands fragment of John, for instance, has been designated P^{52}. The Chester Beatty Library collection in Dublin includes P^{45} of the Gospels and Acts, P^{46} of the Pauline epistles, and P^{47} of Revelation. P^{66} is the Bodmer Library's papyrus of John. P^{72}, a third-century papyrus of Jude and 1 and 2 Peter, and P^{74}, a seventh-century papyrus of Acts and the Catholic Epistles (James; 1 and 2 Peter; 1, 2, and 3 John; and Jude), are also

P[46], a papyrus manuscript in the Chester Beatty Library collection, is one of the earliest known texts of Ephesians. This fragment contains Ephesians 1:1-11. (Used by permission of the University of Michigan Library.)

in the Bodmer Library. None of the books of any of the papyri is complete; many pages are damaged or missing in all of them.

Uncial Manuscripts. Although papyrus manuscripts of the New Testament are written in uncial letters, the term "uncial manuscript" is used to designate only *parchment* manuscripts written in uncial letters.

Although papyrus was still used for secular literature until about the seventh century, Christians began using parchment in the first half of the fourth century, just about the time when the Emperor Constantine gave Christianity official recognition in the Roman Empire in A.D. 325.

In recognizing the Christian religion, Constantine ensured that it would no longer be treated as an illegal and subversive movement. Christians were freed to worship openly and build church buildings. Moreover, the Christian scriptures no longer had to be concealed for fear of confiscation, and copying them no longer had to be done in secret by people who were sincere Christians but were not professional and experienced scribes. Now the manuscripts of the New Testament could be copied openly and officially, although individual Christians continued to make their own copies as well. Indeed, in A.D. 331 the Emperor himself ordered that fifty copies of the Bible be made for the churches of Constantinople, his capital city. In A.D. 350 some old and damaged papyrus codices in the famous library of Pamphilus in the city of Caesarea were replaced by parchment copies.

Parchment manuscripts have been found in many parts of Europe and the Middle East. A very few are now in the United States.

About two hundred years ago it became customary to designate uncial manuscripts by capital letters. When all the English letters had been used, the capital Greek letters that differ from English letters were used. Even this addition yielded a total of only thirty-seven letters, however, so the same letter was sometimes used for two or more manuscripts that contained different books of the New Testament; for example, one Codex D of the Gospels and another Codex D of the Pauline epistles. In 1844 the German scholar Constantin von Tischendorf discovered the manuscript now known as Codex Sinaiticus in the Monastery of St. Catherine on Mount Sinai. He was so impressed with this manuscript's importance that he did not want to have an insignificant letter assigned to it. Since the first letter of the English and Greek alphabets had already been used, he insisted on designating his new discovery by the first letter of the Hebrew alphabet, ℵ (aleph), which has given headaches to writers and printers ever since!

As the number of uncial manuscripts coming to the attention of scholars increased, it became clear that a less limited type of designation was necessary. In 1890 Caspar René Gregory devised the system by which uncial manuscripts are now designated. Under this system uncial manuscripts are identified by a number prefixed by a zero (e.g., 02, 048, 0250). The manuscripts that were already identified by a letter, however, are still commonly referred to by their letter designation, even though they have been assigned an identifying number as well. Under this system, Codex Sinaiticus is Codex 01, which would have made Tischendorf happy.

Among the better-known uncial manuscripts are the following:

Codex Aleph (01), Codex Sinaiticus, is now on display in the British Museum. Written about A.D. 350, it originally contained the Old Testament, the New Testament, and some other Christian writings. This large manuscript (about 15 by 13-1/2 inches) contains four columns of writing on each page. It is one of the most important manuscripts of the New Testament. It was taken from Mount Sinai by Tischendorf and presented to the Czar of Russia. In 1933 the British government purchased it for about $500,000 that had been raised by private donations.

Codex A (02), Codex Alexandrinus, written in the fifth century, is on display beside Codex Sinaiticus in the British Museum. It was presented to the King of England in 1627 by the Patriarch of Alexandria, Egypt, which is the basis for its name. It originally contained both the Old and New Testa-

Codex Sinaiticus (א, 01). This folio contains Mark 1:1-35. (Used by permission of the Trustees of the British Museum.)

ments, written two columns to the page in an attractive and more formal handwriting than that of Codex Sinaiticus.

Codex B (03), Codex Vaticanus, has rested in the Vatican Library for many centuries. Written about the middle of the fourth century, it is the most important single manuscript of the New Testament. This manuscript, too, contained both testaments, written three columns to the page.

Codex D (05), Codex Bezae (meaning "of Beza," because it once belonged to the scholar Theodore Beza), is a sixth-century manuscript that features Greek and Latin on facing pages. It contains the Gospels and Acts, written one column to the page. It is located in the library of Cambridge University. Another Codex D (06), Codex Claromontanus, containing the Pauline epistles, is located in Paris.

Codex Ξ (the Greek letter Xi) (040), Codex Zacynthius (the Latin form of Zante, the Greek island from which it came), is an eighth-century palimpsest owned by the British and Foreign Bible Society in London. It originally contained only the Gospel of Luke, but it is unique in that it is the oldest known New Testament manuscript in which a very extensive commentary of quotations from various Church Fathers appears. This "catena," as the commentary is called, is written in smaller handwriting than the text of Luke, and in a different style of uncial letters. In the thirteenth century the manuscript was taken apart, damaged sheets were discarded, and the rest were erased. The sheets were then cut at the fold and refolded in the usual four-sheet quires to make a new book half the original size. The text of this later book is a "lectionary," a type of manuscript we will discuss shortly.

Codex N (022), Codex Purpureus Petropolitanus ("the Purple Manuscript of St. Petersburg"), located in Leningrad, together with Codices O (023) in Paris, Σ (Sigma) (042) in Italy, and Φ (Phi) (043) in Greece, are a group of four elegant manuscripts containing the Gospels written in silver ink on parchment dyed purple.

A good many manuscripts are, like Codex Sinaiticus, quite large, and many others are at least as large as a good-sized modern book in page dimensions. In addition to the manuscripts themselves, reproductions of various types have been made of a few of the more important manuscripts and can be seen at certain libraries.

Minuscule Manuscripts. A far larger group of New Testament manuscripts comprises those written in minuscule handwriting, dating from the ninth century to the invention of printing, and a few even later. Most minuscules are written on parchment, although some of the latest are written on paper. Like uncial manuscripts, the earlier minuscule manuscripts are generally more carefully written and have less ornamentation than those of later centuries.

About 2,600 minuscule manuscripts are presently known to exist. They are designated by number (e.g., Cod. 23, Cod. 457, Cod. 2035).

Since most of the minuscules were copied later than the uncials, they are generally more copies removed from the originals than are most of the uncials and therefore may be expected to have more variations from the original text. This is not always the case, however. A twelfth-century manuscript might be only ten copies from the original while an eighth-century manuscript might be twenty copies from the original. Indeed, Codex 33, a ninth-century minuscule manuscript containing most of the New Testament, has such a reliable text that it has been called "Queen of the Cursives" (i.e., of the Minuscules). Codex 1, a twelfth-century manuscript, is probably the best manuscript of the half-dozen or so that were used to prepare the first Greek New Testament to be published after the invention of printing. Codex 565, in the public library of Leningrad, is one of the most beautiful of all New Testament manuscripts. Prepared for "the Empress Theodora," it is written in gold letters on purple parchment.

Lectionaries. Very early in the Christian era certain sections of the New Testament were selected for reading in services on each day of the year. Some New Testament manuscripts have indications in their margins of the beginnings and endings of these sections. Before long, however, these passages were assembled in the order in which they were to be read, and were copied in that order in manuscripts called "lectionaries," or lesson books. One type of lectionary contains a passage for every day of the year, beginning with Easter; the other type contains readings for Saturdays and Sundays only. Most of the passages are introduced by one of seven or so fixed phrases that fits the passage, such as "The Lord said to his disciples," "The Lord said," "At that time," and "Brothers." The majority of the lectionaries contain passages from the Gospels, but many contain passages from the epistles, and some include both Gospels and epistles.

About two thousand lectionaries are known, the earliest consisting of fragmentary manuscripts from the sixth century written in uncial letters. Most, however, are from the minuscule period.

Lectionaries are designated by the letter "L" or the abbreviation "Lect." followed by a number (e.g., l225, Lect. 1280).

The number of known Greek manuscripts of all types amounts to more than five thousand, written from as early as the middle of the second century to as late as the end of the fifteenth century, and varying from part of one sheet to the entire New Testament. No other writing from ancient times even begins to compare with the New Testament in the number of manuscripts that have survived to the present.

Even so, witnesses to the text of the New Testament do not stop with this mass of Greek manuscripts. Let us look further.

Versions

In ancient times, books were not usually translated from one language into another. In the few instances in which translation was done, the result was usually so loose and free a rendering that it would be of little use in determining the exact words of the original.

The first significant departure from this type of loose translation was in the translation of the Hebrew Old Testament into Greek over an extended period between about 250 and 150 B.C. According to a fanciful ancient tradition, the ruler of Egypt became interested in the Jewish religion and wanted to read the Jewish scriptures, so he consulted with elders of the Jews and requested them to have a translation made into Greek. The elders then selected six scribes who knew Greek from each of the twelve Jewish tribes. Each of these seventy-two scribes was put into a separate room and assigned the task of translating the entire Old Testament. At the end of the allotted time of seventy-two days, the scribes were brought out, their translations were compared, and it was found that each of the seventy-two translations was identical to the others word for word! This gave confirmation to the Egyptian ruler that the Jewish scriptures were surely from God.

Although this story is obviously unhistorical, the tradition does account for the name given to this translation. It is called the *Septuagint*, from the Latin word for "seventy" (shortened from "seventy-two" for convenience); it is often designated by the Roman numeral symbol for seventy, LXX. At least two other translations of the Old Testament into Greek were made, but the Septuagint is the best-known and is the translation to which the New Testament writers commonly referred when they quoted the Old Testament in the New Testament books. It is also the form of the Old Testament of Codices Sinaiticus and Vaticanus.

Almost as soon as the New Testament books were written, the Gospel was being preached to people of other languages, and there was consequently a need to translate the New Testament into these languages. The translations that were produced have likewise come down to us in the form of ancient manuscripts. These translations, or versions, were faithful renderings, and they are therefore useful to us in textual criticism of the New Testament. Of course the value of a version for textual criticism is not so much the text of the version itself as the light that it sheds on the Greek text from which the version is translated. In addition, since the approximate date when the version was made is usually known, as is the general geographic area or country in which it was made, the versions give us helpful information about the particular form of the Greek text that was read and known in that location at that period of time.

Since Latin was the language of Rome, a Latin translation of the New Testament was needed very early in the missionary work of the young Christian church. It is likely that several translations into Latin were made before the end of the second century, because the surviving manuscripts differ from one another almost too much to have come from a single original translation. This early Latin is known as the Old Latin, or the Itala. The manuscripts of the Old Latin that have come down to us indicate that this version was used at least to some extent until the ninth century or later.

As the Roman church became more important, and particularly after Christianity gained official status in the Roman Empire, the Latin New Testament became more important, and the variety of readings in the Old Latin manuscript became more troublesome. Finally in A.D. 382 Pope Damasus commissioned Jerome, the outstanding Bible scholar of the day, to revise the Latin Bible to make it agree with the Greek text more closely. With the later help of other scholars, this new Latin version was completed after some years. It became known as the Latin Vulgate, meaning the "common Latin" version, and to this day it remains the official version of the Roman Catholic Church.

The Latin Vulgate was a translation that could be understood by the ordinary people who spoke Latin. Yet as time passed and the Latin language changed and other languages developed from it, the Latin Vulgate Bible was not altered or revised. Within a few centuries, this version that had been made to enable ordinary people to read the Bible had become a book that only priests and scholars could understand. The church authorities, moreover, were by that time declaring that it was dangerous for the lay people to read the Scriptures, lest they develop heretical ideas from them.

The influence of the Latin Vulgate is indicated by the fact that no fewer than eight thousand manuscripts of the Vulgate New Testament are known today, more than all the known Greek New Testament manuscripts of every type combined. This great number, coming from every century from the fifth to the fifteenth, reflects the fact that for many centuries the Bible of the Christian church was the Latin

Bible. During much of this period, Greek was little known and its importance little recognized outside of Greece.

Syriac, a language closely related to the Aramaic that Jesus and his disciples spoke, was the language of some of the countries neighboring Palestine. Syriac, too, needed a translation of the New Testament in the very early days of the Christian church. It is possible that the Gospels were first translated from the Greek original into Syriac during the middle of the second century in the form of the *Diatessaron* (meaning "through the four"), a version that sought to combine all four Gospels into one continuous account. This work is credited to a man named Tatian, but we have little direct knowledge of it.

The New Testament was probably translated into Syriac during the second century. Two manuscripts of parts of the New Testament in this Old Syriac, as it is called, are known today. A Syriac version called the *Peshitto* (meaning "simple"), which is still the recognized Syriac New Testament, was made about the beginning of the fifth century. The Peshitto did not contain 2 Peter, 2 or 3 John, Jude, or Revelation, since the Syriac church did not at that time accept these books as canonical (i.e., as part of the inspired New Testament text). These books were later supplied from subsequent Syriac translations called the *Philoxenian* and the *Harkleian*.

During the past few years some individuals have made much of the fact that Syriac is closely related to Aramaic. Claims have been made that the Syriac New Testament is the "genuine" New Testament, written in the language that Jesus spoke. One proponent of this view published a New Testament "from Eastern sources" and succeeded in impressing many people with its importance. More recently, a manuscript of the Syriac Peshitto was carried around the United States with great ceremony (one state governor took his oath of office with one hand on an English Bible and the other hand resting on this manuscript!) and with claims that the manuscript represented the New Testament in its original language. But even if Syriac and Aramaic were the same language—which they are not (for one thing, they were written with completely different alphabets)—the fact remains that the New Testament was originally written in Greek, and the

New Testament in any language other than Greek is a translation from the original Greek and is thus one step removed from the original.

The Gospel was carried to Egypt, too, at an early period, and the New Testament was translated into several dialects of the Egyptian language over an extended period of time. This language, called Coptic, was written in a combination of Greek letters and some additional symbols that were needed to indicate Coptic sounds that did not occur in Greek. A translation into the Sahidic dialect of Coptic, spoken in the southern part of Egypt, was made in the second century; the translation into Bohairic, the dialect of Alexandria and the north, may not have been made until the third century.

Other early versions have some significance for New Testament textual criticism. One of these is Gothic, spoken by tribes near the Danube River in Europe; the New Testament was translated into Gothic by Bishop Ulfilas in the fourth century. The Armenian translation of the New Testament was made in the fifth century using an alphabet newly developed for this language by a monk named Mesrop. This same Mesrop is credited with developing a special alphabet for the translation of the New Testament into the Georgian language as well, which was spoken by the people of the region between the Black and Caspian Seas. Finally, the Slavonic version is credited to two brothers named Cyril and Methodius, who were missionaries during the ninth century in what is now Bulgaria. Cyril is credited with the invention of one form of the Slavic alphabet, which is called Cyrillic in his honor.

Of course, we do not have the original manuscripts, or even near originals, of any of these versions. In order to use these versions to help us know the Greek text from which they were made, we must first apply principles of textual criticism to the existing manuscripts of the version to determine as nearly as possible what the original text of the version was.

Patristic Quotations

The final major source of our knowledge of the text of the New Testament is the quotations of the New Testament found in the writings of the ancient Christian writers commonly called the Church Fathers. The writings are known as "patristic" (from *pater*, Latin for "father"). Most of the Church Fathers wrote in Greek or Latin, but some wrote in Syriac and a few other languages.

The New Testament quotations in these patristic writings are remarkably extensive. Indeed, it has been said that the whole New Testament could be reconstructed from these patristic quotations alone.

As in the case of the versions, we know when and where each of the Church Fathers lived, and so the form in which a Father quoted a New Testament passage can show us the textual form in which the passage was known in a given location at a particular time. These references must be examined with special care, however, to determine whether the writer copied the quotation directly from a manuscript, recalled it from memory (in which case differences could be attributed to inaccuracies of memory rather than textual differences in a manuscript), or was making a reference or allusion that was not intended to be a direct quotation.

As with the versions, we do not have the original manuscripts of the Fathers' writings, so principles of textual criticism must be applied to the later copies in order to determine as nearly as possible the exact form of the Fathers' original writings and of the quotations contained in them.

Some of the more important Greek Church Fathers are Irenaeus, Bishop of Lyons (second century); Clement of Alexandria (second and third centuries); Origen of Alexandria and later of Caesarea (third century); Eusebius Pamphili of Caesarea (fourth century); John Chrysostom ("John Goldenmouth," so named for his eloquence) of Constantinople (fourth century); and Cyril of Alexandria (fifth century). The Latin Fathers include Tertullian (second and third centuries); Jerome (fourth and fifth centuries), who was responsible for the Latin Vulgate Bible; and Augustine (fourth and fifth centuries).

CHAPTER FOUR

The New Testament through the Centuries

We have looked into the way in which the New Testament books were written and noted the forms in which the New Testament has been preserved. Now let us take up the ways in which the manuscripts of the New Testament were copied and passed on through the centuries to bring the Word of God to us.

This is a very important aspect of our study, because no matter how accurate the books of the New Testament may have been in their original form, we do not have these original manuscripts. What we know about the contents of the New Testament comes from copies many times removed from the original manuscripts, copies made at various times through many centuries. We should face the fact that if these copies do not furnish us with the true text of the New Testament, we have no way of knowing what the authors actually wrote, no matter how important their message may have been. It would be very dangerous to say as some people do that in certain passages the manuscripts agree but that the original text must have been different and was lost in the process of copying. Such proposals open the door to changing the scriptural text virtually anywhere it does not agree with the reader's prejudices. We must trust that the same Holy Spirit who inspired the original text was able to protect it through the centuries of handwritten copying.

As Christians, we believe that the Holy Spirit guided the authors of the New Testament books so that their message would be protected from error. As 2 Peter 1:21 puts it, "as they were moved by the Holy Spirit, men spoke from God." We likewise believe that the Holy Spirit operated providentially in the copying and preservation of the manuscripts through the centuries. At the same time, we should not think that it was only by supernatural preservation that the New Testament was kept from being lost or hopelessly confused during those centuries. Many other ancient books were copied and recopied down through the years, and although some of them have been lost, many others have come down to us in reliable form. Even on merely human presuppositions there is no reason to believe that the New Testament as we have it today is not fully reliable, accurately representing the original text.

Although the process of copying ancient manuscripts was basically the same for the New Testament as for secular literature, there were nevertheless some differences, especially during the two and a half centuries before Christianity gained official recognition in the Roman Empire. The secular classics were usually, though not always, copied by professional scribes and checked against accepted copies or originals by professional proofreaders. The New Testament, on the other hand, was probably copied during this earliest period mostly by ordinary Christians who were not professional scribes but who wanted a copy of a New Testament book or books for themselves or for other Christians. They did not have the same opportunity as the secular copyists to compare their manuscripts with other manuscripts because of the persecution that was often near at hand and that kept them from displaying their scriptures too openly. In addition, copying a book by hand was a slow and tedious task; probably very few early Christian families possessed an entire New Testament.

As we noted earlier, hand-copying a manuscript of more than two or three pages, no matter what its text, will almost certainly involve making some changes from the original.

This is all the more likely to be true in Greek texts, in which no spaces are inserted between the words. As a result, probably no two manuscripts of a New Testament book or any other ancient book are absolutely identical in words, spelling, and other details. Moreover, as scribes copied these copies, and other scribes copied their copies, they continued to make changes through the centuries. Most of these changes were insignificant; those that were of importance—the ones with which we are concerned—were introduced during the first two centuries after the New Testament was written.

This being the case, how can we be confident that the New Testament has been faithfully preserved for us? Some years ago a popular magazine published an article proclaiming that New Testament scholars admitted that the New Testament as we know it today may contain as many as fifty thousand errors! Such a preposterous statement was the result of sheer ignorance by the author of the article. I later learned that he had consulted with at least one New Testament scholar but had badly misunderstood what he had heard. He was doubtless told that if we could count *all* the differences of *every* type in *all* the thousands of New Testament manuscripts, they might amount to fifty thousand. Yet even these hypothetical fifty thousand differences between the manuscripts would not all be errors, since the differences would include the correct readings as well as the incorrect ones.

Let us look more closely at this great number of differences between the manuscripts. One of the largest groups of these "variants," as they are called, includes differences or errors in spelling. For example, the common Greek spelling of "John" uses a double *n*, but one good manuscript spells it with a single *n*. Differences like these are of no significance for meaning, and we can disregard them.

A second very large group of variants involves other changes in the Greek text that make no difference in meaning. Many of them entail differences in the Greek for which there is no real counterpart in the English language. For example, in Greek a person's name can be written either with or without the Greek equivalent of "the" preceding it, whereas in English we do not say anything like "the Andrew saw the

Jesus." As another example, in Greek the phrase "the good man" can also be written "the man the good," but in English both phrases could only be translated as "the good man."

A third type of variant is less common, involving instances in which the scribe accidentally makes nonsense of a phrase or writes a word that is clearly incorrect. Copying Luke 6:41, for example, one scribe accidentally wrote the Greek letter *pi* instead of *phi,* making the verse read "Let me take the *fruit* out of your eye" instead of "Let me take the *speck* out of your eye"! As a more recent example of such a blunder, I have a copy of an early edition of the "Good News for Modern Man" New Testament (TEV) in which the entire last chapter of 2 Peter is omitted and "Philippians" is misspelled at the top of every page of that epistle!

The textual variants that concern us, of course, are those that affect the meaning of the New Testament in some way. There are a few thousand of these, but we should be clear on the fact that they affect only a small portion of the New Testament text. If twenty manuscripts of a book of the New Testament were selected at random and distributed to twenty people who could read them, any person in the group could read from his manuscript and the others would have no trouble in following him in their manuscripts. Indeed, the verbal agreement between the various New Testament manuscripts is actually closer than the verbal agreement between many English versions of the New Testament.

As we look at the textual variants that affect the meaning of the text to some extent, we will find that some are fairly important while others are less so. In addition, for some variants it is easy to decide which is the correct reading, while in other instances it is very difficult. However, we can be certain that no truth of Scripture or Christian doctrine rests on a doubtful text.

In dealing with these variants, both the important and the less important ones, there are principles to guide us in making our decisions. We will be discussing these in a later chapter. These principles do not give absolute answers for every variant, but when they are properly applied they reduce the amount of the New Testament text that remains in serious doubt and is of real significance for meaning to something less than an average of one word in a thousand.

The Development of "Families" of Manuscripts

Since copying manuscripts by hand tends to bring errors and changes into the copies, the New Testament books came to differ more and more among themselves as they were copied and recopied. This divergence was not merely random, however; rather, it resulted in a kind of grouping of the manuscripts into families or, as they are sometimes called, "text-types." Nor do we mean to imply that the divergences continued to accumulate so that later manuscripts become quite unreliable. Rather, the introduction of textual variants soon reached its maximum, after which additional errors and differences were largely attributable to a given scribe working on one or a few manuscripts.

Let us now look into how the families of manuscripts, or text-types, arose. Keeping in mind that this explanation is oversimplified, let us suppose that four copies are made from an original manuscript and that each of these copies has its own distinctive differences from the original. As further copies are made from each of the four, each further copy will contain most of the peculiarities of the copy that preceded it, although scribes might notice and correct some of the changes. In this way the copies made from each of the four will tend to be more like the other manuscripts of their "family" than like the manuscripts copied from any of the other three initial copies. All of them will contain the same basic text, but the manuscripts of each of the four families will share distinctive readings in which they differ from the manuscripts of the other three families. In addition, within each of the four families the manuscripts that are nearer to each other in the process of copying will be even more similar to one another. In other words, it is somewhat like the human race, in which all people look alike in general but each racial group has its own distinctive features, and close human relatives tend to resemble each other even more closely.

Although we cannot be certain of some details, it appears

Autograph

As this diagram indicates, the path from autograph to extant manuscripts can be complicated; for instance, a given manuscript may have been copied from two different manuscripts. Nevertheless, as more and more copies of copies were made, families of manuscripts began to develop.

that at a very early date after the New Testament was written, some copies were multiplied in Palestine, and other manuscripts were taken to various regions, including Alexandria, Constantinople, and Rome. In each of these localities further copies of the manuscripts were made. These copies contained readings distinctive of these groups and differing from the manuscripts produced in other localities, although all manuscripts agreed except in these details. Today we recognize four principal groups of manuscripts, or text-types: the Alexandrian, the Byzantine (for Byzantium, another name for Constantinople), the Caesarean (for the city of Caesarea in Palestine), and the Western (for Rome). In addition, there are numerous manuscripts and a few versions that cannot be classified as belonging to any of these groups. In general this situation was established by the time Christianity gained official recognition by the Roman emperor in the early part of the fourth century.

With the official recognition of the Christian religion by

the Emperor Constantine there came a new freedom to copy and compare manuscripts of the Bible on a more professional basis. As manuscripts were compared more freely, and especially as manuscripts from various geographical regions were compared, Christians began to realize that there were differences between them. This evidently led to some attempts to bring the manuscripts into greater agreement by making changes in the existing manuscripts themselves or by making changes as the manuscripts were copied. This was not done in any really thorough manner, however, nor by following any well-developed principles. It appears that preference was often given to the readings of Constantinople, since that city was then the center of the Greek-speaking church. This process of making changes and corrections continued for perhaps three centuries or so, with the result that the readings characteristic of Constantinople (the Byzantine readings) became the generally accepted form of the biblical text, and the readings characteristic of other regions were largely neglected. Of the manuscripts that are now known, almost all of those from the eighth century and later are Byzantine in their readings, and these comprise some ninety-five percent of all presently known manuscripts.

The statistics do not mean that the Byzantine manuscripts, or the Byzantine text-type, are either more correct or less correct than the manuscripts of other text-types, any more than the facial features of a family of ten children who resemble one another are more "correct" than those of a family of only one child. Indeed, if the number of known manuscripts were the deciding factor in determining the preferred text, we would have to follow the Latin Vulgate, for there are more known manuscripts of that version than of all the Greek manuscripts of all four text-types together. Our decision concerning the merits of each text-type will have to await our discussion of the guiding principles we must follow.

CHAPTER FIVE

The New Testament Meets the Printing Press

In the middle of the fifteenth century an event occurred in Europe that revolutionized the Western world of literature. In 1454, in the German city of Mainz, Johannes Gutenberg invented a method of printing from movable type. With this invention it became possible for the first time to print any number of identical copies of a book or other document and to print them with a rapidity beyond comparison with the snail's pace of hand-copying.

In China it is claimed that printing from movable type has been carried on in that country since A.D. 1041, with the invention credited to a man named Pi Sheng. Because of China's isolation from the Western world, however, this development had no influence in Europe. It was only through Gutenberg's genius that this remarkable process was made available in the West. Its significance for our civilization is almost beyond comprehension.

As the printing press of Gutenberg and his partner Fust was followed by more and more such presses across Europe, the age of manuscripts, in their literal meaning of "handwritten" copies, drew to a end. Not every scribe immediately laid down his pen and joined the ranks of the unemployed or learned to set up printer's type, of course. Some hand-copying continued for many years. Yet the invention of printing from movable type, which we take so completely for granted, marked the beginning of a new age, an age in which the distribution of books was no longer dependent upon copies tediously produced one at a time with no two copies exactly alike—an age in which the very possession of books would no longer be the virtual monopoly of the wealthy.

The first item that came from the press of Fust and Gutenberg was an ecclesiastical indulgence, a single-sheet document produced for Roman Catholic church authorities. The first Bible was produced two years later, in 1456. This first of all "first editions" was a Latin Vulgate Bible, since at that time scholars had very little interest in the Greek text, and the Vulgate was the Bible of the church. This edition, now known as the Gutenberg Bible, was a beautiful edition of "folio" size—about sixteen inches in height and twelve inches in width. About forty copies are known to be in existence today.

It took more than half a century before the Greek New Testament was printed, and it involved the very earliest example of lively competition in the publishing industry. In 1502 the Roman Catholic Cardinal Ximenes of Toledo, Spain, began to prepare an edition of the Greek Bible. He arranged to have the Old Testament printed with the Hebrew, Latin, and Greek texts in parallel columns. The Latin text was to be placed in the center column, the Cardinal's editors stated, "just as Jesus hung on the cross between two thieves"! The New Testament had the Latin and Greek texts in parallel columns.

The New Testament of the Cardinal's edition was actually off the press and ready for distribution in 1514, but the decision was made not to publish it—that is, not to make it available to the public—until the Old Testament volumes were ready. When the Old Testament was printed, publication was further delayed until the Pope gave the necessary approval. Although this approval came in 1520, the books were apparently not actually available for sale until 1522. This Bible came to be known as the *Complutensian Polyglot*, *Complutum* being the Latin name for the city of Alcala, where it was produced, and *polyglot* meaning "many tongues," referring to the three languages of the text.

Cardinal Ximenes's edition was thus the first Greek New

Testament to be printed. But it was not the first to be published and placed on the market. A Swiss printer named Froben, a Protestant, heard of the Cardinal's project and promptly sought out the scholar Desiderius Erasmus to ask him to prepare an edition of the Greek New Testament as quickly as possible. Erasmus had been anxious to publish a Greek New Testament and readily accepted Froben's proposal.

Froben made his request in April 1515. In July Erasmus went to Basel, Switzerland, hoping to find Greek manuscripts in a library there that would be good enough for the printer to use in setting up the type for publication of the text. He could not find a manuscript containing the entire New Testament, so he used about half a dozen manuscripts of various books of the New Testament. Where more than one of his manuscripts contained the same part of the New Testament, he made some comparison of their readings and made some changes here and there where he felt it was necessary. For the book of Revelation, Erasmus had only one manuscript. This manuscript had lost its final leaf, which contained the last six verses of the book, and in other passages the biblical text was confused with a commentary on the text that was intertwined with it. In these verses Erasmus simply made up his own Greek text, translating it from the Latin. As a result, some words in his text of Revelation have never been found in any Greek manuscript!

As quickly as possible, Erasmus presented his New Testament text to Froben, who hastened to set it in type and get it into the press. The edition was completed and placed on the market early in March 1516, less than a year after the project was initiated.

This first edition of Erasmus's Greek New Testament, a large folio volume of about a thousand pages, did not contain the reference to the "heavenly witnesses" in 1 John 5:7-8. His Greek text read "For there are three that bear witness, the spirit, and the water, and the blood; and these three agree." For several centuries, however, the Latin Vulgate had read "For there are three that bear witness in heaven, the Father, the Word, and the Holy Spirit; and these three are one. And there are three that bear witness on earth, the spirit, and the water, and the blood; and these three agree." As a result of this difference between the texts, one of the Catholic editors of the Complutensian Polyglot criticized Erasmus for omitting this reference to the "heavenly witnesses," which of course is a strong affirmation of the Trinity. Erasmus responded that the passage was not contained either in the Greek manuscripts he had used or in any Greek manuscript he had examined after preparing his text. However, he finally rashly promised that if he could be shown any Greek manuscript containing the "heavenly witnesses" he would include it in a future edition of his New Testament.

Not long afterward, a Greek manuscript was shown to him that did contain the passage. It is now known that the manuscript was prepared by a Franciscan friar in Oxford specifically for the purpose of showing it to Erasmus; he simply made a Greek translation from the Latin Bible and inserted it at the proper place in the Greek text.

Erasmus strongly suspected that he had been tricked, but he nevertheless fulfilled his promise and inserted the "heavenly witnesses" in his third edition of 1522, with a footnote indicating his doubts about the manuscript that had been shown to him. In his fourth and subsequent editions he again omitted the passage. By a quirk of circumstances, however, it was Erasmus's third edition that proved to have the most lasting influence on other editions by other editors, and thus the reference to the "heavenly witnesses," which is not found in any Greek New Testament manuscript produced earlier than the sixteenth century, came to be an accepted part of the Greek text and later found its way into the King James Version in English. Incidentally, the manuscript that was used to twist Erasmus's arm is Codex 61, now located in the library at Trinity College in Dublin, Ireland.

Before continuing with our story, it may be well to note that the absence of the reference to the heavenly witnesses in 1 John 5:7 does no harm to the scriptural doctrine of the Trinity. Indeed, the scribe who first inserted these words centuries ago did so because he already believed the doctrine of the Trinity. The New Testament contains abundant testimony that the one true God exists in three persons, Father,

Son, and Holy Spirit. All three persons of the Trinity are mentioned together in passages such as Romans 15:30, "through our Lord Jesus Christ and through the love of the Spirit . . . in your prayers for me to God"; 1 Corinthians 12:4-6, "Now there are diversities of gifts, but the same Spirit; and there are diversities of ministries, but the same Lord; and there are diversities of operations, but the same God"; and 2 Corinthians 13:13, "The grace of the Lord Jesus Christ and the love of God and the fellowship of the Holy Spirit be with you all."

When the Complutensian Polyglot finally became available in 1522, Erasmus examined it and realized that at some points its text was preferable to his own. Because of this, in his fourth edition of 1527 he adopted some readings from the Complutensian. Yet the Complutensian Polyglot never had the influence on editors of subsequent editions that the work of Erasmus did. This was partly because Erasmus had had the advantage of getting his edition on the market before the Complutensian and partly because his edition was less expensive and was printed in a more convenient form.

Other editors soon began publishing the Greek New Testament. Most of these editors consulted the text of Erasmus, and they often virtually reprinted it as their own, since there were no copyright laws to protect an author's work—and sometimes few scruples on the part of the publisher. As we noted earlier, it was Erasmus's third edition that these other editors most commonly used, even though his fourth edition contained numerous improvements.

One of these other editors was Robert Estienne, a member of a family of printers in Paris and later Geneva. Under the name Stephanus, the Latinized form of his family name, he published four editions of the Greek New Testament between 1546 and 1551. A noteworthy contribution of his fourth edition was the introduction of the verse numeration that we still use today. Our chapter divisions had been developed about 1205 by Stephen Langton, Archbishop of Canterbury.

Two brothers of the Elzevir family of Holland published seven editions of the Greek New Testament between 1624 and 1678. They, too, borrowed heavily from the text of

Erasmus. Among other features of their editions for which we are indebted to these brothers is the phrase "Textus Receptus," or "Received Text," the phrase commonly used to refer to the Greek text of Erasmus and his followers. This phrase was first used by the Elzevir brothers in their second edition, published in 1633. In this edition they stated optimistically—in Latin, of course, as any good scholar did in their day—"You have therefore the text now received by all, in which we give nothing altered or corrupt."

In any case, we should note that this Greek text of Erasmus and the editors who followed him was by no means a precise text faithfully preserved from the original manuscripts of the New Testament. Rather, it was based largely on Erasmus's hasty comparison of a few manuscripts of no unusual value that he happened to find in the university library in Basel. He did have one tenth-century manuscript, Codex 1, which was older and had a better text than did his other manuscripts—but the fact that its text differed from that of his other manuscripts made him doubt its value, and so he did not make much use of it.

Of course Erasmus ought not to be blamed for his failure to appreciate the value of Codex 1, since neither he nor anyone else of his day had any understanding of the nature of textual variants and their significance or of the principles by which the correct readings can be determined.

The Textus Receptus did indeed become the generally "received text" for nearly three hundred years, as well as the basis for the translation of the early English versions, including the King James, and various versions in other European languages. It is by no means a "poor" or "bad" text. In fact it is about as good, or reliable, as the average ancient manuscript of the New Testament. It gives us the whole Word of God. Yet in numerous details it is not as close to the exact original text as are the best of the ancient manuscripts, and it is certainly inferior to the best text that can be determined by a proper comparison of the manuscripts using sound principles of procedure.

CHAPTER SIX

More Manuscripts,
and What They Revealed

The publication of the Greek New Testament in multiple copies on the printing presses contributed to a renewed interest in the New Testament in its original language. This interest, in turn, stimulated the publication of still more editions of the Greek New Testament to satisfy the increased demand. Indeed, by 1633, little more than a century after the first edition was published, a hundred editions of the Greek New Testament had appeared, almost all of them closely following the texts of Erasmus and Stephanus. Gone was the day when a complete New Testament was the prized possession of only a few libraries, churches, and wealthy individuals. Now almost anyone who desired a copy could purchase one.

The Increasing Demand for a Better Text

This increased interest in the Greek New Testament now began to cause scholars to give attention to the many ancient manuscripts of the Greek New Testament that were to be found in the libraries of Great Britain, Europe, and the Middle East but that had lain neglected in the past.

As scholars began to give more attention to these manuscripts, studying and comparing them with the printed text, they came to see more and more that there were many differences among the manuscripts and between the manuscripts and the printed texts. They were forced to begin to evaluate these differences and to try to determine which manuscripts had the readings that were more likely the correct original text.

In the meantime, the printed text, since it was better known than the text of the manuscripts, came to be regarded by many people as the true original New Testament text, which therefore should not be tampered with. As scholars continued their work, however, more and more ancient manuscripts came to light and were examined, and more and more instances were found in which the readings of the manuscripts differed from the reading of the printed text. Some scholars became convinced that the Textus Receptus could be improved by replacing its text in numerous passages with readings from the manuscripts. Some even advocated setting aside the Textus Receptus altogether and making a new beginning based on a comparison of manuscripts.

Beginning early in the eighteenth century, new editions of the Greek New Testament began to be published, editions that were no longer simply reproductions of the text of Erasmus and Stephanus. One of the first of these was that of the English scholar John Mill. His edition, published in 1707, made only a few changes in the Textus Receptus. He did, however, make a significant contribution to the study of the text by including footnotes—which are now called a "critical apparatus"—containing many readings from seventy-eight manuscripts, some ancient versions, and a number of quotations from the Church Fathers. These notes made it easy for readers to see how these other sources differed from the Textus Receptus and to make comparisons for themselves. Even so, Mill was roundly criticized for tampering with the commonly accepted New Testament text.

In 1734, the German scholar J. A. Bengel published a Greek New Testament in which he made a few cautious changes in the Textus Receptus. In his critical apparatus he indicated additional readings that he believed were preferable to the reading of the Textus Receptus but that he did not actually put into his text. Another important contribution Bengel made was to classify the manuscripts he had studied into two groups based on the similarity of their textual variants. This grouping of related manuscripts was an important new concept in the study of the manuscripts.

Each manuscript is generally given a name or number based on the system of cataloging used in the library in which it is kept. A manuscript might be designated by a title such as "Papyrus Oxyrhynchus 2834," for example, or "Bibl. Nat. Gr. 222." It would be awkward to have to use such lengthy designations in a critical apparatus in which many manuscripts must be named repeatedly, however. To resolve the problem, in his 1751-52 edition of the Greek New Testament, J. J. Wetstein assigned a capital letter to each uncial manuscript and an Arabic number to each minuscule manuscript, as we noted in Chapter 3. Wetstein then published a list that identified the manuscripts by the capital letter or number and by their local library identification. For example, the library designation for Codex B is Vat. Gr. 1209, for Codex 33 is Bibl. Nat. Gr. 14, for Codex 565 is Egerton 2785, and for Codex 225 is Vind. Suppl. Gr. 97.

Following the lead of Bengel and his classification of the manuscripts into two groups, other scholars moved away from treating each manuscript separately and toward arranging the various witnesses to the text—Greek manuscripts, versions, and quotations from the Church Fathers—into groups of texts that are closely related. J. S. Semler proceeded to identify three families instead of Bengel's two, calling them the Alexandrian, Western, and Eastern, reflecting to some extent the geographical areas in which he believed they had originated. Semler also listed a great number of textual variants in his editions, indicating the witnesses that supported each reading and giving his opinion as to which reading was the original text.

During this period, which extended from about 1633 to 1830, many manuscripts were read and collated. To "collate" a manuscript is to read it and compare its text with another text, normally a printed text that is generally available to other people (commonly the Textus Receptus), recording in a concise list the differences of the manuscript from the printed text. By using the collation together with the printed text, the reader could get the full text of the manuscript without having to consult the manuscript itself. And of course the collation makes clear where and how the manuscript differs from the printed text.

The Displacement of the Textus Receptus by the "Examined Text"

Although more and more evidence was being collected that indicated that the Textus Receptus needed to be improved and corrected at many points, it was not an easy matter to make the necessary changes. Very few people had any understanding of the manuscripts or the significance of the textual variants. Most people who knew anything about the Greek New Testament knew only the Textus Receptus, and many of these considered it to be the true original text that must not be altered—just as in our own day many people have loudly protested the publication of English New Testaments other than the King James Version. The scholars who dared to make even a few changes from the Textus Receptus in their editions of the New Testament were severely criticized. Still, there was a continuing increase of evidence that the Textus Receptus did not fully represent the original text as the inspired authors had written it, and that the original text could be more nearly represented by substituting certain readings from other manuscripts. This evidence could not be ignored forever.

Finally, in 1831 a German scholar, Karl Lachmann, dared to publish an edition of the New Testament he prepared from his examination of manuscripts and variants, deciding in each case what he believed the original reading was, independently of the Textus Receptus. Unfortunately, he did not include in his edition any explanation of the principles he had followed in preparing his text, except to state that in a certain little-known theological journal he had written an article explaining his principles. He could hardly have succeeded better in opening himself and his text up to criticism! Lachmann was a Greek scholar, not a theologian, and so he may not have realized what strong feelings surrounded the Textus Receptus. At any rate, a few years later he published a second edition of his New Testament, this time with a full explanation of the principles he had followed in producing his text and in deciding between textual variants. His explanation finally silenced some of the criticism against his work and won support for his text.

An English scholar, Samuel Prideaux Tregelles, published a Greek New Testament during the period from 1857 to 1879 that was likewise independent of the Textus Receptus. He used fairly sound principles, which he explained clearly. His edition contained an extensive critical apparatus showing which manuscripts, versions, and patristic quotations supported his text in each instance in which he had chosen between two or more readings in the manuscripts. This clear presentation, together with his personal reputation and his recognized experience in working with the Greek manuscripts, helped to encourage acceptance of his edition.

One of the greatest names in New Testament textual studies is that of Constantin von Tischendorf. It would take a book to describe his career. Probably no other person has discovered and made known the text of as many Greek New Testament manuscripts as did this nineteenth-century scholar. In addition to many others, he read and published a text of an important palimpsest manuscript, Codex C, which is located in the National Library of Paris. The original New Testament text of this manuscript was written in the fifth century and then erased some years later to receive the text of some of the works of the ancient Church Father St. Ephrem. For this reason it is known as Codex Ephraemi Rescriptus, "the rewritten codex of Ephrem."

Far more significant was Tischendorf's discovery of the famous Codex Sinaiticus in the monastery of St. Catherine on Mount Sinai, the text of which he also published. Altogether Tischendorf made available to the world the text of more than forty manuscripts from libraries in various parts of Europe and the Middle East.

In addition to his manuscript studies, Tischendorf found

time to publish no fewer than eight editions of the Greek New Testament between 1841 and 1872. His eighth edition consists of two volumes containing the New Testament text together with a vast and detailed critical apparatus, and one volume of extensive descriptions and identifications of manuscripts. The "eighth major edition," as it is called (to distinguish it from a one-volume condensation known as the eighth minor edition), contains an immense amount of information about manuscripts and their textual variants. A century after it was published it is still a necessity for serious study of the manuscripts of the New Testament and their readings.

Tischendorf produced his eighth edition independently of the Textus Receptus. Its text is somewhat weakened by its heavy dependence on the readings of Codex Sinaiticus, which he had discovered a few years earlier, but the great and enduring value of this monumental work is its critical apparatus and its vast amount of information concerning manuscripts.

All of the editions we have noted had their influence in bringing people, little by little, to accept the fact that the Textus Receptus was simply one form of the Greek text and not necessarily the closest possible text to the original.

In 1881-82 one further edition of the Greek New Testament was published that climaxed the long struggle against the domination of the Textus Receptus. This edition brought general recognition of the principle that the original text of the New Testament should be determined by studying the many variants in the manuscripts and applying sound principles to make decisions. This watershed edition was the Greek New Testament published by two British scholars, Brooke Foss Westcott and Fenton John Anthony Hort. They spent twenty-eight years preparing the edition, which was published as a two-volume work, one volume containing the New Testament text and one volume entirely devoted to an explanation of the principles they had followed. Their text had an immediate practical effect: while they were preparing their Greek text they made it available to the committee that was preparing the English Revised Version of the Bible, with the result that this English New Testament, which was published in 1881, includes many of their choices of readings rather than the Textus Receptus readings found in the King James Version.

The principles that Westcott and Hort used and supported were not completely new, of course. They learned from the scholars whose work had preceded theirs, and they built on these foundations. Some aspects of their principles have subsequently been modified by many scholars. It is widely believed, for example, that they leaned too heavily on readings of the Codex Vaticanus (Cod. B) in their text. Nevertheless, on the whole their work remains a landmark in New Testament textual studies.

Scholars continue to differ in their decisions concerning many textual variants in the manuscripts. Some still insist that the Textus Receptus is not only the best text, but that it alone is the Word of God. But it is important to see that the inspired, authoritative New Testament has come down through the centuries in a great multitude of ancient manuscripts that differ from one another in various details, that almost all of these manuscripts give us the Word of God, and that the exact wording of the original text can be determined only by studying the variants and applying sound principles to decide among them.

And now, let us look at these important principles.

CHAPTER SEVEN

Determining the Correct Reading

We have noted that in hundreds of words and phrases of the New Testament the ancient manuscripts, the versions, and the quotations from the Church Fathers differ among themselves. In some instances there may be only two readings—that is, there may be only two choices of words. In other instances there are several readings, occasionally as many as eight or ten. Since this is the case, what hope is there that we can determine what the New Testament text actually is? How can we know what the inspired writers actually wrote?

In the first place, it is important to remember that even with the great number of variants, the manuscripts still agree in most of their text. In the second place, where there are variants, most of them do not affect the meaning of the text. Very few variants give meanings that are actually false, except for occasional scribal blunders found in one manuscript or a few; we will deal with these a bit later.

The reason for studying the manuscripts, then, is not to decide whether the New Testament does or does not teach certain basic truths but rather, for the most part, to decide small details and relatively minor matters. Someone might ask, then, why we should bother at all if no important truths are at stake. The answer is that the New Testament is of such supreme importance that if careful study will enable us to make our text even slightly closer to what the New Testament writers wrote, or if it will enable us to see that our New Testament is already as nearly identical with the original text as it can be made, it will be worth the effort.

Most people, of course, have no ability to study the Greek manuscripts and must simply accept one or more translations or versions in English or whatever their language is. This is quite proper. These readers are accepting the decisions of those who made the translation they are reading. Even these readers, however, will often wonder about differences they find between the various versions. How do we go about deciding between the differences in the manuscripts to determine which is most likely the original text?

"Internal Evidence" and the Basic Principle

The first and most basic principle of textual criticism is this: *The reading from which the other readings could most easily have developed is most likely the original.*

Let's look at one class of examples of this principle. In many passages in the Gospels, some manuscripts of one Gospel agree almost word for word with another Gospel while other manuscripts differ somewhat. One such instance is found in the story of the rich young ruler. Mark 10:17-18 and Luke 18:18-19 agree in reading " '*Good* teacher, what should I do that I may inherit eternal life?' And Jesus said to him, 'Why do you *call* me good? No one is good except one, *God*.' " In Matthew 19:16-17 some manuscripts are identical with Mark and Luke, while other manuscripts read " 'Teacher, what *good thing* should I do that I may obtain eternal life?' And he said to him, 'Why do you *ask me about what is good?* There is *only one* who is good.' "

Which of these forms did·Matthew write? Both forms are reasonable, and both are theologically acceptable. If Matthew originally wrote the form of the text that is identical with Mark and Luke, there is no apparent reason why a scribe should change it in a later manuscript. If, however, Matthew wrote the form that differs slightly in wording from Mark and Luke, a later scribe might easily have changed the text of Matthew to agree with the other two Gospels. He might have done so unintentionally if the form in Mark and Luke were more familiar to him, or he might have done so intentionally to make Matthew agree more closely with the other two. We conclude, then, that the reading from which the other reading most likely originated is the reading that differs slightly from that of Mark and Luke.

To give another example, Mark 6:47 reads that the boat was "in the middle of the lake." In the parallel in Matthew 14:24 some manuscripts read "in the middle of the lake," while other manuscripts read "many furlongs distant from the land." The meaning of the two readings is essentially the same and no theological issue is involved. If Matthew originally had the same phrase as Mark, there would be no reason for a later scribe to change it; but if Matthew originally had the phrase that is slightly different from that in Mark, a scribe could have changed it to bring it into closer agreement with Mark. Once again, the reading in Matthew from which the other reading most likely arose and which is therefore surely the original, is the reading that differs slightly from Mark.

Scribal changes to make a passage of Scripture agree more closely with a parallel passage are called "harmonizations." This type of change occurs frequently in the Gospels, and most often the instances are the result of attempts to bring Matthew or Luke into closer harmony with Mark. A few instances, however, occur elsewhere, as in the similar passages of Ephesians 1:7 and Colossians 1:14. The Ephesian passage reads "in whom we have the redemption through his blood, the forgiveness of trespasses, according to the riches of his grace." In the Colossian parallel most manuscripts read "in whom we have the redemption, the forgiveness of sins," but a few manuscripts insert "through his blood," as in Ephesians. This phrase does have theological significance. It is included in both Ephesians and Colossians in the Textus Receptus and in the King James Version, but it is not included in Colossians in most of the recent versions in English.

Did Paul include "through his blood" in Colossians as he did in Ephesians? Did a scribe add the phrase because he remembered the similar verse in Ephesians and thought Colossians was the same? Did a scribe deliberately omit the phrase from Colossians because he objected to the doctrine of the blood atonement?

Let's look at the last alternative first. The manuscripts that do *not* have "through his blood" in Colossians 1:14 read "having made peace through the blood of his cross" in 1:20 and include "through his blood" in Ephesians. Why should a scribe object to the mention of Christ's blood in one verse and not object to it a few verses later or in the parallel in Ephesians? We can conclude that the phrase was not omitted deliberately through theological prejudice.

Which form of Colossians 1:14, then, is most likely original? If the reference to the blood was originally in both epistles, there would be no apparent reason for a scribe to eliminate it from Colossians and leave it in Ephesians. On the other hand, if Paul did not include it in Colossians, a scribe could easily have added it later, either intentionally borrowing it from Ephesians or unintentionally confusing it with the Ephesian parallel and inserting it thinking that the phrase had been accidentally omitted from the manuscript he was copying.

We conclude, then, that Paul included the phrase "through his blood" in Ephesians 1:7 but that it was added by a later scribe in Colossians 1:14 and that translators should therefore not include the phrase in Colossians.

Should the presence of harmonizations raise doubts about the accuracy and inspiration of the New Testament, in particular the Gospels, in which most of them occur? Not at all. For one thing, the Gospels differ from one another on every page, even where there are no textual variants. To cite just one example, in Matthew 15:28 Jesus says to the Syro-Phoenician woman, "O woman, great is your faith; let it be done to you as you wish," whereas in Mark 7:29 he says, "For this word, go; the demon has gone out of your daughter." These differences merely reflect the fact that the Holy Spirit operated differently through each writer's personality rather than inspiring them all to express themselves in the same words.

This basic principle—namely, that the reading from

which the other readings could most likely have developed is probably the correct reading—has some further implications. One of these implications is that in many instances *the more difficult reading is likely to be the original*. This statement needs to be qualified a bit, however. What we mean is that if one reading seems at first sight to be unexpected or difficult to understand, but on further study is seen to make good sense, then this reading is probably original.

Let us look, for example, at John 1:18. Many manuscripts, and most English versions, read "No one has ever seen God; the only begotten *son*, who is in the bosom of the father, has set him forth." Many good manuscripts, however, read "the only begotten *God*." In the Greek manuscripts the difference between "God" and "son" is a matter of only one letter. Either reading clearly refers to Jesus. The Textus Receptus reads "son," and certainly no scribe wishing to weaken the text would change it to the much stronger "God." "Only begotten son" makes good sense, and a scribe would have no reason to change it to clarify it. On the other hand, "only begotten God" is unexpected and strange. A scribe could easily have thought that it was a mistaken repetition of "God" from the beginning of the verse and that if he changed "God" here to "son" he would be correcting an error in the manuscript he was reading.

But can "God" be the correct reading here? Does it make sense that John would have written it? Yes, it does. Jesus is referred to as "God" elsewhere in the Gospel of John—in John 1:1, for example—and of course Jesus is called "only begotten" in John 3:16. If we accept the reading "only begotten God" here, the sense of the verse is "No one has ever seen God (the Father); the only begotten One, who is himself God (in his nature), who is in the bosom of the Father, has made the Father known to us." This makes good sense and is in the spirit of much else in this Gospel.

In this passage, then, the seemingly harder reading is preferable, and is the reading from which the other reading could easily have developed.

Of course a "hard" reading is sometimes an obvious error. Readings of this type are usually found in only one or a few manuscripts. We noted earlier that the scribe of one manuscript accidentally changed "speck" to "fruit" in Luke 6:41. Another error of this type occurs in a variant reading of Mark 14:31, in which Peter boldly says to Jesus, "Even if it is necessary for me to di : with you, I will by no means deny you!" But one very old manuscript changes the order of one word and changes a Greek short *e* to a long *e*. As a result, this manuscript has Peter timidly saying "If it is not necessary to die, I will by no means betray you"! Both of these examples are "harder readings," of course, but no great amount of study is required to see that they are merely scribal errors.

The principle of preferring the reading from which the other readings most likely arose has another corollary. This second application of the principle has two parts. The first part is that *the shorter reading is generally preferable* if the difference between the readings resulted from an *intentional* change by a scribe. The reason for this is that scribes of the earliest manuscripts occasionally added a word or a phrase to clarify a thought, but they rarely omitted words or phrases intentionally.

An example is found in the story of the Prodigal Son in Luke 15. In 15:18-19 the son says that he will say to his father, "Father, I have sinned against heaven and before you. I am no longer worthy to be called your son. Make me as one of your hired servants." In some manuscripts, verse 21, in which he actually meets his father, includes the final sentence "Make me as one of your hired servants," but other good manuscripts omit this final sentence. Which reading is correct?

If Luke did not include the additional sentence in verse 21, a later scribe could easily have done so. The scribe might have felt that since the son had said that he would say to his father "Make me as one of your hired servants," he must have said it. Or the scribe might have added it unthinkingly simply because it was included in verse 19. On the other hand, if this sentence was a part of the original text of verse 21, there is no apparent reason for a scribe to omit it, since it accords perfectly with the context. Someone might suggest that the scribe intentionally omitted this sentence in verse 21 because he felt it unnecessary to repeat everything that had appeared in verses 18-19. But study of the manuscripts indicates that scribes simply didn't work that way. The evidence suggests that the shorter reading is doubtless the original, even though good manuscripts include the longer reading.

The second part of the corollary is almost the reverse of the first. This part is that *the longer reading is often preferable* if the difference between the readings resulted from an *unintentional* or accidental change by a scribe. We know that scribes would occasionally skip a word, a phrase, or an entire line as they were copying. This type of error was particularly likely to occur when the same combination of letters appeared twice close together in a line or directly above or below in the next line of the text being copied from. For example, 1 John 2:23 reads "Everyone who denies the son does not even have the father; he who confesses the son has the father also." In the Greek text, the last three words in each part of the verse are "has the father." Some manuscripts omit the entire second half of this verse; a scribe copying the passage obviously let his eye slip fom the first "has the father" to the second and omitted everything between the two phrases. Indeed, in the King James Version the second half of this verse is in italics, indicating that this clause was not in the Greek text from which the King James Version was translated. However, the clause is surely original.

Occasionally the opposite error will occur: a scribe will have let his eye skip back from the second occurrence of a word (or even a repeated letter or letters) to the first occurrence, with the result that the intervening words or letters will be written twice. I myself committed this error in English on one occasion; in trying to copy the words "Newberry Library" from a paper I was typing, I found I had written "Newberry Librerry Library."

In 1 Thessalonians 2:7 the difference between the two readings "we became gentle" and "we became infants" is only the difference between one *n* and two. The question is whether there was originally one *n* and the scribe copied it twice or whether there were two and he overlooked the second one.

Although much of what we have just been discussing

involves intentional changes, by far the most frequent changes are those a scribe made unintentionally. It is important to remember that the oldest Greek manuscripts were written in letters somewhat like capital letters and that words were run together without spacing. Consider the problems of reading page after page written something like this: INTHEBEGIN NINGWASTHEWORDANDTHEWORDWASWITHGODAND THEWORDWASGODTHISONEWASINTHEBEGINNING WITHGOD. In addition, with the differences between various scribes' styles of handwriting, several letters could be confused with one another, such as those in the following groups: ЄΘOC, ΠΓΙΤ, ΑΔΛ, and ΗΝ. The possibility of confusion was increased by the fibrous surface of a papyrus sheet or even irregularities in a parchment leaf.

An example of possible confusion of letters can be seen in 1 Timothy 3:16, in which the difference between "God was manifested" and "he who was manifested" is merely two small horizontal lines: $\overline{\Theta C}$ and OC. In 2 Peter 1:21, the difference between "men spoke from God" in some manuscripts and "holy men of God spoke" in other manuscripts is only the difference between ΠΟ and ΓΙΟΙ.

If a Greek manuscript was being translated into another language, such as Latin or Syriac, there are occasional passages in which the scribe could mentally divide the Greek words incorrectly and translate a different meaning from what the author intended. For example, the English sentence ISAWABUNDANCEONTHETABLE could be read either as "I saw abundance on the table" or "I saw a bun dance on the table." In Mark 10:40 Jesus says, "But to sit at my right hand or my left is not mine to give, but it is for those for whom it is prepared." Some ancient translators took the Greek letters *all ois*, "but for whom," as one word, *allois*, "for others" (since of course there was no space between the letters) and translated the latter part of the verse as "but it is prepared for others."

A mistake in hearing could also lead to an unintentional error. This type of error could occur either if someone were reading a manuscript to a group of scribes as they copied or if a scribe were pronouncing the words to himself and forgot what the written form was. For example, in 1 Corinthians

13:3 the difference between "give my body to be burned" and "give my body that I may glory" is the difference between only two Greek letters that could easily be confused. As another instance, from very early times the Greek words for the plural pronouns *you* and *we* were pronounced alike. There are numerous confusions of these two words in the New Testament manuscripts, as in 1 John 1:4, in which some manuscripts and versions read "your joy" and others read "our joy."

At times a word is unintentionally changed to another word of similar appearance and meaning. In particular, a less common word may be changed to a more familiar word. For example, many English-speaking people reading the sentence "I know the man who is the vicegerent of the company" would say "viceregent" instead of "vicegerent." In Revelation 1:5 the author doubtless originally wrote "loosed us from our sins." However, since he adds "by his blood," which suggests washing, a scribe accidentally or intentionally added one letter to the middle of the Greek word, which changed it from "loosed" to "washed." In this case the change was to a word of similar appearance rather than to a more familiar word. If the end of the verse had read "by his cross" instead of "by his blood," the change probably would not have been made.

We see, then, that internal evidence is very important in deciding between differences in the readings of the manuscripts. At the same time, there are limits to the application of internal evidence. For one thing, scribes are human beings and do not always act in completely predictable ways. It is sometimes impossible to deduce how a certain variant developed or what the original reading is on the basis of internal evidence. Beyond this, scholars may differ both in their interpretation of how a variant developed and in their conclusions concerning the original reading.

Happily, there is an additional means for helping us to determine the original text of the New Testament that involves using the manuscripts themselves to aid in the decision. It is called "external evidence."

External Evidence

As we said earlier, four large groups of New Testament manuscripts, called "text-types," have been identified—the

Alexandrian, the Western, the Caesarean, and the Byzantine. (The Caesarean has been identified only in the Gospels, which leaves only three principal groups in Acts, the epistles, and Revelation.) The manuscripts in each of these text-types agree with one another more closely than with the manuscripts of any other text-type and tend to share peculiar readings or errors. The situation is somewhat similar to the differences between the racial groups of mankind and the shared characteristics within each racial group.

At the same time, the manuscripts of a given text-type do not agree with one another completely. Within each text-type there are smaller groups that agree with one another still more closely. Even within these smaller groups no two manuscripts will be exactly identical. Here, too, the situation is analogous to that of subgroups and families within the races of mankind.

Sometimes a text-type will be divided, with its manuscripts supporting two different readings almost equally. Some manuscripts will in some instances agree with one text-type and in other instances agree with another.

In order to use these groups of manuscripts to help us determine the original reading in variants, we will need to decide how reliable each text-type is, ranking them from most to least reliable. By "most reliable," we mean, of course, the text-type that most often seems to have the correct reading among textual variants. In making this determination, we will base our decisions on readings that appear in most of the representatives of that text-type, overlooking peculiar readings of only one or a few manuscripts of the group.

In order to determine the relative reliability of the text-types, we might examine a large number of variants (in a Gospel, or in several epistles, or even in the entire New Testament), selecting only variants in which internal evidence points rather clearly to the correct reading. For each of these variants we could then note which text-type or text-types support that reading. The results of such an examination would reveal that the Alexandrian is the most reliable text-type, followed by the Caesarean, the Byzantine, and the Western, in that order.

Of course, no single text-type is always correct and none is always wrong, but such an examination gives us an additional basis for determining the original reading among textual variants. Other things being equal (although they often aren't!), we will usually trust the more reliable text-types over the less reliable ones. At the same time, we will usually favor a reading supported by more than one text-type over a reading supported by only one text-type. This means that at times we will have to choose between a reading supported by one good text-type and a reading supported by more than one less reliable text-type.

With this additional data we can return to an examination of variants with two basic questions to ask: first, "On the basis of internal evidence, which reading is the one from which the other reading or readings most likely developed?" and second, "On the basis of external evidence, which reading is supported by the most reliable text-type or text-types?"

Armed now with both internal and external evidence, we can examine the variants with added confidence. In some instances, both internal and external evidence will support a reading—that is, it will be the reading from which the other readings most likely developed, and it will be found in the best text-types. In other instances, we will not be able to decide which reading gave rise to the others, but external evidence will clearly point to one reading. In still others, the manuscript evidence will be almost equally divided, but internal evidence will indicate fairly clearly which is the reading from which the others probably developed. Sometimes, unfortunately, internal and external evidence may seem to be contradictory, or neither will give a clear indication; in these instances a decision will have to be tentative and doubtful.

Now let's look at an example of each of these four situations.

In Matthew 5:47 some manuscripts read "Do not even the gentiles do the same?" while other manuscripts read "tax collectors" instead of "gentiles." The preceding verse reads "Do not even the tax collectors do the same?" It is therefore likely that the correct reading in verse 47 is "gentiles" and that a scribe changed it to "tax collectors" either unintentionally or to make it agree with the similar statement in the preceding verse. There is no apparent reason for a scribe to have changed "tax collectors" to "gentiles" here. Internal evidence therefore favors "gentiles" as the original reading. Looking at external (manuscript) evidence, "gentiles" is supported by the Alexandrian, Western, and part of the Caesarean text-types—that is, by two and a half text-types, including the best and part of the second-best type; "tax collectors," on the other hand, is supported by the Byzantine and part of the Caesarean text—that is, by one and a half text-types, including part of the second-best plus the third best. External evidence thus clearly supports "gentiles." In this variant, then, both classes of evidence combine to support the same reading.

In John 5:44, in the phrase "and the glory which is from the only God you do not seek," the word "God" is omitted in many of the manuscripts of the Alexandrian text-type, giving the sense of "from the Only One," which of course would still mean God. The word "God" is included in the other three text-types. This means that the best text-type is opposed by the three other text-types, which leaves a decision uncertain. Looking at internal evidence, we note that in the Greek manuscripts "God" would have been written as $\overline{\Theta Y}$ in the sequence TOYMONOY$\overline{\Theta Y}$OY. In light of the combination of similar-appearing letters, we might suppose that a scribe could easily have omitted these two letters accidentally. Furthermore, although a scribe might have added "God" for clarity if it was not in the original, it is unlikely that John would have failed to include the word "God" in this passage, in which God is so prominent in the discussion. In this variant, then, external evidence is not decisive, but internal evidence is rather clear.

In Matthew 7:24, on the other hand, internal evidence is not decisive but external evidence is clear. The variant is between the phrase "he shall be likened to a wise man" and "I shall liken him to a wise man." There is little difference in meaning, and internal evidence does not give much help. "He shall be likened," however, is supported by the Alexandrian and most of the Caesarean and Western texts, whereas

"I shall liken him" is supported primarily by the Byzantine text. "He shall be likened" is thus clearly favored by external evidence, while internal evidence is indecisive.

Finally, regarding a variant in Matthew 15:38 internal and external evidence seem contradictory. At least part of each of the four text-types supports the reading "apart from women and children," while there is much weaker support for "apart from children and women." On the other hand, the phrase "women and children" is the more normal order, and it occurs a bit earlier in the text, in Matthew 14:21. It seems very unlikely that a scribe would have changed the more usual "women and children" to the more unusual "children and women," but a scribe could easily have changed "children and women" to "women and children." So internal evidence favors "children and women" as the original reading. In this passage, then, external evidence favors one reading while internal evidence favors the other reading.

Let us remind ourselves again, however, that most variants entail only small differences or no differences in meaning, and that very few variants involve readings that are doctrinally erroneous except for occasional scribal blunders that can easily be recognized.

Characteristics of the Text-Types

We have noted that assessing external evidence is an important part of deciding which is the correct reading among textual variants. In making use of this external evidence, it will be additionally helpful if we know some of the characteristics of each text-type—specifically, what kinds of readings each text-type tends to include, and also what kind of errors it tends to make and what kind of wrong readings it tends to accept. Knowing the kinds of errors a text-type is prone to include will help us to be suspicious in cases in which it appears to have a reading of that kind.

Let us consider first the Alexandrian text-type. As we have noted, it is generally the most reliable of the text-types; however, neither it nor any other text-type is always correct. When the Alexandrian has a wrong reading, it is often a "sophisticated" change (i.e., an intentional change) rather than a careless mistake. For example, in Romans 5:1 the Alexandrian text supports the reading "let us be having peace," while the other texts support "we have peace." The difference between these two readings is merely the difference between a long o and a short o in the Greek verb "have." The correct reading is probably "we have peace." An Alexandrian scribe might have thought that "being justified by faith" implied that we do have peace with God and that Paul would not have in effect repeated himself by saying "we have peace" but rather would have said "let us be having peace"—that is, "let us continue to enjoy the peace we have received"—and the scribe might then have changed his manuscript accordingly. Other considerations in the verse substantiate the contention that "we have peace" is the original reading.

Another example of this sort of thing occurs in the story of the Prodigal Son in Luke 15:21, which we have already looked at. A large number of the Alexandrian manuscripts mistakenly add "Make me as one of your hired servants," probably on the assumption that the son did in fact say to his father all that he said he would in verse 19.

On the other hand, the Alexandrian text includes readings that are abrupt or terse but that prove to be correct, as well as readings that at first sight seem more difficult to understand than the alternative readings but that on further study make good sense. One example is the phrase "in order that everyone who believes may in him have eternal life" in John 3:15 instead of "in order than everyone who believes in him may have eternal life" (which is the text of the following verse). Another example is the reference to Jesus as "only begotten God" instead of "only begotten son" in John 1:18.

Characteristics of the Byzantine text include readings that provide smoother transitions, are easier to understand, or are theologically stronger than the alternatives. For example, the Byzantine text of Mark 7:5 reads "unwashed" hands, while the alternative reading is a word that can mean either "unwashed" or "ceremonially unclean." The Byzantine text of Mark 1:2 reads "the prophets," while other manuscripts read "Isaiah the prophet," since the passage quotes both Malachi and Isaiah. The Byzantine also contains many more readings than other text-types in which one Gospel passage is harmonized to agree with the parallel in another Gospel.

The Western text frequently has a reading that is different from but similar to alternative readings; for example, "praising God" instead of "blessing God" in Luke 24:53 and "a hundredfold" instead of "manifold" in Luke 18:30. In addition, in Acts the Western reading is often a rewording of alternative readings. For example, in Acts 3:11 most manuscripts read "And while he was holding on to Peter and John, all the people ran together to them in the portico," but the Western text reads "And as Peter and John were going out, he went out together with them holding on to them; and they, amazed, stood in the portico."

The most puzzling type of Western reading involves omissions of a sentence or part of a sentence, especially in Acts and the final chapters of Luke. (Some scholars say that in these passages the Western text is the original and the other text-types have made additions, but most scholars consider this to be unlikely.) For example, the Western text omits the angel's words "He is not here, but he has risen" in Luke 24:6, although it includes these words in Matthew 28:6. The Western text also omits the phrase "blood and fire and vapor of smoke" in Acts 2:19.

As for the Caesarean text, it does not seem to have strong unique characteristics but agrees sometimes with the Alexandrian and sometimes with the Western text, although it does not follow the long paraphrases and omissions of the Western text.

Some Witnesses to the Four Text-Types

The most important witnesses to the Alexandrian text include the papyrus codex P[66] (which was written about A.D. 150 and is one of the two oldest known New Testament manuscripts), P[75], Codex Aleph (Sinaiticus), Codex B (Vaticanus), and Codex 33, as well as the Bohairic version of Egypt and the quotations of Cyril of Alexandria.

The Western text is contained in Codex D (05) of the Gospels and Acts (Cod. Bezae), Codex D (06) of the Pauline epistles (Cod. Cantabrigiensis), and the Old Latin version.

The Caesarean text is found in Codex Theta (known as the Koridethi Gospels, an uncial manuscript); in Codex W (Cod. Washingtoniensis) of Mark from chapter 5 on; in Family 1 and Family 13 (two groups of minuscule manuscripts closely related to Cod. 1 and Cod. 13 respectively); in the Georgian, Armenian, and Palestinian Syriac versions; and in the Gospel quotations of Cyril of Jerusalem.

The Byzantine text is supported by most of the uncial manuscripts of the fifth century and later, by most of the minuscule manuscripts, and by most of the versions and Church Fathers of the fifth and later centuries.

Did Scribes Intentionally Corrupt the New Testament Text?

To admit, as we have, that scribes at times made intentional changes in the manuscripts they were copying may raise fears in the minds of some people that scribes may have deliberately falsified or watered down the text of the New Testament in some passages. We need have no such fears. The scribes who copied the New Testament manuscripts, especially in the earliest period when most of the variants developed, were doing so because they wanted to make the message available to more readers, not to change it. In later centuries, scribes were often monks who were copying the manuscripts as part of their religious duties, often without really understanding the Greek they were copying. These later scribes were hardly in a position to introduce subtle heresies into their manuscripts. I have personally examined some seven or eight thousand New Testament variants with a good deal of care, and I would be hard pressed to make even a brief list of variants that give evidence that a scribe was attempting to weaken or falsify the message.

There were men in the early church who did, in fact, attempt to distort the New Testament text. One of these was the second-century teacher Marcion, who totally rejected the Old Testament and made numerous changes in the epistles to suit his own views. Marcion and others like him were not scribes, however; they were teachers. They did not advance their views by copying manuscripts incorrectly, even though they may have made changes in their own New Testaments. They depended instead upon teaching and publicizing their doctrines. Scribes, on the other hand, were not engaged in studying the text but simply in copying it.

CHAPTER EIGHT

Looking at Some New Testament Variants

Let us now look at some New Testament variants, using both internal and external evidence. We will generally refer to text-types rather than to individual
manuscripts in considering external evidence.

In dealing with the variants in the following pages, it will
not be practical to present a detailed evaluation of the external evidence in making our decisions, since this evidence is
often complicated and not easily presented in the brief form
we need to use. Instead, we will simply try to discern the
conclusion toward which the external evidence points. Our
guidelines concerning this external evidence will be in accord
with what we noted earlier about the reliability of the text-
types: no text-type is infallible, but in general their order of
reliability is first the Alexandrian, then the Caesarean, the
Byzantine, and the Western. In addition, support by more
than one text-type is preferable to support by only one text-
type, other things being equal. Moreover, a text-type should
be suspect when it has a variant reading involving the type
of error it frequently makes.

Variants with Little Difference in Meaning

The great majority of textual variants involve little or no
difference in meaning. They are of importance primarily to

the scholar who is studying details of the text, but they also help show us that most of the changes scribes made were *not* included for the purpose of changing the meaning of the text. Let us sample some variants of this type.

In Matthew 12:15 some manuscripts read "many crowds" (i.e., "great crowds") where others read simply "many," who followed Jesus. If simply "many" is original, a scribe might have added "crowds," since "many crowds" is a common expression in the Gosels; but if "many crowds" is original, there would seem to be no good reason for a scribe to omit "crowds." In this instance, then, the internal evidence favors "many" as the original reading. When we look at the external evidence, we find that the support for "many" is good but not decisive, leaving the decision in doubt. Since internal evidence favors "many" and external evidence is doubtful, we will accept "many" as the original. The difference between the two readings is, of course, virtually nothing.

In Matthew 22:30 some manuscripts read "they are as angels in heaven," while others read "they are as angels of God in heaven." If "angels of God" was original, there is no apparent reason for a scribe to have omitted "of God"; but if "angels" was original, a scribe could have added "of God" to make the identification more specific. Internal evidence thus favors the shorter reading, "angels." As for external evidence, both readings have some support from three text-types, but the support for "angels of God" is much more extensive. In considering both types of evidence together, the reasoning behind internal evidence seems strong enough for us to accept its conclusion in spite of the greater external support for the longer reading. So we conclude that the original reading was simply "angels." Once again, the sense is the same for either reading.

Luke 4:17, which states that Jesus "opened the scroll" of the prophet Isaiah, offers a tantalizing variant. The readings involve the two verbs "opened" and "unrolled." "Unrolled" is an appropriate word to use with reference to a scroll, which is what Jesus was reading. If "unrolled" is original, a scribe might possibly have changed it to "opened" because that word is more common (the word "unrolled" occurs nowhere else in the New Testament) or because he was thinking of a book in codex form, which would be opened rather than unrolled. On the other hand, if "opened" was original, it is possible but less likely that a scribe would have changed it to the specific word for opening a scroll, "unrolled"; indeed, a related word meaning "rolled up" occurs in verse 20. Internal evidence therefore appears to favor "unrolled" slightly. In external evidence, "unrolled" has good support from all text-types except the Alexandrian and appears to be favored slightly, even though the best text-type supports "opened." In conclusion, both lines of evidence appear to favor "unrolled" slightly, and so we will accept that meaning. Once again, the difference involves only a technical detail of meaning.

In Matthew 8:25 the question is whether the disciples cried "Lord, save!" as some manuscripts read or "Lord, save us!" as other manuscripts read. Considering internal evidence, if "us" was in the original, a scribe would hardly have omitted it, whereas if the original was the more abrupt "Lord, save!" a scribe could easily have added "us" either unthinkingly or intentionally. In external evidence, "save" is Alexandrian and Caesarean, while "save us" is Western and Byzantine. Thus, both lines of evidence support "Lord, save!" without the addition of "us." Again, the meaning is the same for both readings.

In 2 Thessalonians 2:3, did Paul write "man of sin" or "man of lawlessness"? Both words make good sense. "Sin" is a much more common word in Paul's writings than is "lawlessness," however, and a scribe is more likely to have changed a less common word to the more common one than vice versa. As for manuscript evidence, support for "lawlessness" is limited to the Alexandrian text-type, whereas "sin" has much broader support. In conclusion, the internal evidence and the Alexandrian manuscript support indicate that "lawlessness" is the original reading. As in the previous examples, there is no essential difference in sense between the readings.

Harmonizations

A class of variants we noted earlier consists of instances in which one passage has been changed to agree with a similar or parallel passage in another book. Most of these are found in the Synoptic Gospels—Matthew, Mark, and Luke—but a few occur elsewhere.

In Matthew 1:25 there are two readings—"until she bore a son" and "until she bore her first-born son." There is no reason for a scribe to have omitted "her first-born" if it was in his text, but a scribe might have added it if it was not in his text. It seems all the more likely that the phrase "her first-born" was added to an original that did not include it because the parallel passsage in Luke 2:7 reads "she bore her first-born son," and a scribe could easily have borrowed the phrase either intentionally or unintentionally from that source. "A son" is supported by a strong part of the Alexandrian and Caesarean texts, whereas "first-born son" has some support from all text-types. The external evidence is therefore rather equally balanced, but the strong internal evidence leads us to accept "a son" as the original text.

The Lord's Prayer in Matthew 6:9 begins "Our Father who is in heaven." In this prayer as recorded in Luke 11:2-4 some manuscripts have the same reading as Matthew while others simply read "Father." Internal evidence indicates strongly that Luke originally read "Father" and that the addition was made under the influence of the text of Matthew and probably from the use of the prayer in public and private devotions. Manuscript evidence for "who is in heaven" is fairly extensive, but the support for "Father" is better. The strong support for the shorter reading by internal evidence plus the external support makes the reading "Father" certain as the original text of Luke 11:2.

In our earlier discussion of harmonizations we dealt with Colossians 1:14. We noted that internal evidence, the evidence of probability, indicates clearly that Paul did not include the phrase "through his blood" when he wrote this verse, but that it was added by a later scribe drawing on the parallel passage in Ephesians 1:7. We can now look at the external evidence for this variant. None of the text-types—not even the Byzantine—supports the inclusion of "through his blood" in Colossians; it appears in only a few individual manuscripts and other witnesses. On the other hand, as we noted in the earlier discussion, all three text-types include "through his blood" in Ephesians, which negates the charge that it was omitted from Colossians in order to weaken the passage theologically.

Although this reading has very little textual support, it did happen to be included in the manuscript of Colossians that Erasmus used in making his Greek New Testament edition in 1516. In this way the phrase came into the Textus Receptus version of Colossians and was then passed on to the King James Version. But internal and external evidence indicate beyond any doubt that although Paul did include the phrase in Ephesians, he did not include it in Colossians.

Some Interesting Variants

Let us now look at some variants that are interesting for one reason or another without being theologically important.

One variant that I believe unnecessarily tantalizes textual scholars is found in Mark 6:22. In this passage concerning the famous dance by the daughter of Herodias that cost John the Baptist his head, one reading refers to the girl who performed the dance as "the daughter of Herodias herself" or "Herodias's daughter herself"; the other principal reading is commonly taken to mean "his daughter Herodias." In addition, a number of versions have simply ignored the pronoun "herself" or "his" and read "the daughter of Herodias." Looking at internal evidence, the first and third readings make good sense; if either of these was original there would have been no reason for a scribe to introduce the second one. The second reading, however, would cause problems, since the girl was not the daughter of Herod, and her name was not Herodias. If this second reading was original, a scribe could easily have been tempted to alter two letters of the Greek pronoun "his" to change the meaning to "herself."

I believe this second reading is the original. It is a "hard" reading, but it is not an error by Mark. Instead of reading the Greek phrase as "his daughter Herodias," we can read it as "his daughter of Herodias," meaning "his daughter—that is, Herodias's" (i.e., "his step-daughter, who was actually the daughter of his wife Herodias"). This construction is admittedly a bit awkward, but I believe that Mark could have written it, and I do not see how the pronoun "his" could have been introduced by a scribe if it were not original.

Turning to external evidence, we find that this reading is supported by the Alexandrian text and Codex D of the Western text, which is strong support—and this in spite of the difficulty the passage might have posed to the scribes who copied it. Since it is also clearly preferred by internal evidence, I am confident that "his daughter—that is, Herodias's" is original.

Luke 6:1-10 deals with the observance of the Sabbath laws. At the end of verse 4, Codex D adds this brief item: "On the same day, [Jesus] seeing someone working on the Sabbath said to him, 'Man, if you know what you are doing, blessed are you; but if you do not know, you are under a curse and a transgressor of the law.' " This story fits the context of the chapter, and the incident may be true, but since it is found in only one manuscript we cannot even consider the possibility of its being a part of the original text.

In Ephesians 1:1, some manuscripts omit the words "in Ephesus." These words could not easily have been omitted accidentally. They could hardly have been missing originally, even though some scholars believe they were; without them the Greek text is awkward. It can be rendered in English fairly acceptably as "to the saints who are also faithful," but this raises the serious question of why Paul would have put this emphasis on the "faithful" saints. Actually the Greek very likely would be "to the saints who are, and faithful," as a reference to the greetings in Philippians 1:1 suggests. Some commentators have suggested that Paul intended that this letter be copied and sent to several churches and that he left a blank space after "are" so that the appropriate destination could be inserted into each copy. However, no other destinations or churches are named here in any known manuscript of this epistle (although the heretical teacher Marcion did call it the epistle to the church in Laodicea). Internal evidence, then, favors the inclusion of the phrase "in Ephesus."

As for manuscript evidence, a good part of the Alexandrian text plus the early papyrus P^{46} support the omission, while the Western, Byzantine, and part of the Alexandrian support the inclusion of the phrase. This might seem to leave the external evidence in doubt. However, as we pointed out in the preceding chapter, the Alexandrian text sometimes makes a "sophisticated" error—that is, an intentional change that has some reason and thought behind it but is nevertheless wrong. This may be such an instance: an Alexandrian scribe, knowing the tradition that this letter was sent to several churches, may have taken it upon himself to omit the designation "in Ephesus." In conclusion, then, although the manuscript support for the omission is good, it is the type of error that the Alexandrian text sometimes makes. Moreover, the support for the inclusion of "in Ephesus" is broader, and internal evidence strongly supports the inclusion.

In Revelation 12:18 the two readings are "I stood on the sand of the sea" and "he stood on the sand of the sea." The difference is only a matter of the inclusion or omission of the Greek letter n. "He stood" fits in with the preceding verses, which refer to the activities of the dragon. "I stood" fits in with the verb "I saw" that follows immediately in 13:1. However, a study of the structure of Revelation shows that the words "And I saw" almost always indicate the beginning of a new section. On this assumption, 12:18 should be the end of the preceding section referring to the dragon, and "he stood" would more likely be the original. As for manuscript evidence, "I stood" is probably Byzantine; "he stood" is clearly Alexandrian and therefore preferred. Thus, both internal and external evidence indicate that the original text is "he stood on the sand of the sea."

In 1 Corinthians 11:29 the two readings entail the inclusion and omission of the word "unworthily" in the verse "For he who eats and drinks [unworthily] eats and drinks judgment to himself, not discerning the body." If "unworthily" was in the original text there would be no reason for it to have been omitted intentionally, since that is clearly the sense of the verse; nor is there any basis for supposing that it would have been omitted accidentally. On the other hand, if "unworthily" was not in the original text, a scribe, thinking that "not discerning" meant *"because* he does not discern" and that the verse would therefore seem to condemn everyone, could easily have added "unworthily." However, "not discerning the body" can also mean "if he does not discern the body," which does not require the word "unworthily." From internal evidence we therefore conclude that the omission is preferred. As for manuscript evidence, "unworthily" is supported by the Byzantine and Western texts, while the omission is supported by the Alexandrian text plus the early papyrus P[46]. Both internal and external evidence thus support the text without "unworthily," with "not discerning the body" meaning "if he does not discern the body."

At the end of the same verse, after "not discerning the body" some manuscripts add "of the Lord." This latter phrase would not easily have been omitted accidentally if it were original; and there would have been no reason for even a heretic to omit it intentionally, since "the body" is clearly the Lord's body. On the other hand, if the phrase was not original, a scribe could easily have added it in order to leave no doubt about the meaning. The manuscripts for and against the addition are almost exactly the same as for the addition and omission of "unworthily." Again, both internal and external evidence agree, and we conclude that what Paul wrote here was "not discerning the body."

Sometimes the scribes have really warmed to their work and have developed a great variety of readings in a particular passage. In Mark 6:33, for example, a considerable assortment of variants for "preceded them" in the phrase "they ran together there and preceded them" have accumulated, including the following: "came to them," "came together there," "came there," "preceded him there," "came together to him," "preceded them and came together to him," and others. Scribes may have made the changes because they felt that it was unlikely that the crowds on foot could have arrived before the boat did.

Colossians 2:2 also has an assortment of readings. The original text is almost certainly "to the true knowledge of the mystery of God, [namely] Christ." However, since it is possible to misunderstand the Greek text as saying "the mystery of God of Christ," scribes apparently tried to clarify the text in various ways, producing such variants as "the mystery of Christ," "the mystery of God and of Christ," "the mystery of God, which is Christ," "the mystery of God who is in Christ," "the mystery of God the father in Christ Jesus," "the mystery of God the father of Christ," "the mystery of God the father of Jesus Christ," "the mystery of God the Father and of Christ," "the mystery of the God and Father of Christ," and "the mystery of the God and Father and of Christ." A careful study of these many readings can show how they developed from the simple original. It is important to note, however, that in this very theologically meaningful passage none of the variant readings show any attempt to weaken or distort the theology.

Galatians 4:7 is another passage in which scribes have developed a multitude of readings. The original text is surely "and if you are a son, you are also an heir through God." It is more natural, however, to think of our being heirs through Christ than through God, although the latter concept is reasonable (cf. 1 Cor. 1:9). This apparent problem led scribes of various manuscripts to change "through God" to "of God," "because of God," "through Christ," "through Jesus Christ," "of God through Christ," "of God through Jesus Christ," "through God in Jesus Christ," and "of God and joint-heir of Christ." Once again, however, not one of these readings shows any attempt to corrupt this theologically significant passage.

Romans 4:19 has a variant of two readings that seem at first to be contradictory: Abraham "considered his own body as already dead," and "did not consider his own body as already dead." The contradiction, however, is only a matter of appearance, not substance. The first reading means that even though Abraham recognized that his body was too old, he nevertheless did not hesitate to believe God's promise that he would have a son. The second reading means that because of God's promise, Abraham did *not* consider his body too old to enable him to become a father. Both readings, then, make good sense, although "considered" requires a bit of thought to understand the argument, while "did not consider" is easier to grasp at first sight. So it is more likely that "considered" was changed to "did not consider" than vice versa. "Considered" is the Alexandrian reading; "did not consider" is Western and Byzantine. Both internal and external evidence, therefore, support "considered." Whichever reading is assumed to be original, however, it is important to note that the change was not an attempt to weaken the text or introduce a false teaching.

It is remarkable how much difference in meaning one small Greek letter can make. In Luke 2:14, for example, if the final word in the Greek text ends with an s, the meaning is "upon earth peace among men of good will." If the final word ends without an s, the meaning is "upon earth peace, good will among men." In the first reading it is possible that "men of good will" could refer to people who have an attitude of good will toward others, but it much more likely means people who are the objects of God's good will (i.e., those with whom he is pleased), as most modern versions interpret the passage.

The question is whether Luke wrote that final Greek s or not. The form without the s is easier to interpret; indeed, its meaning is so obvious that it is very improbable that a scribe would have changed it intentionally. On the other hand, if the s was original, a scribe might have omitted it intentionally to make the reading easier to understand, or he might have omitted it accidentally, since the Greek s at the end of a line was sometimes written as a very small raised letter. Internal evidence, then, favors the reading with the s.

In manuscript evidence, the form with the s is supported by the best part of the Alexandrian and Western texts, while the other form is Caesarean and Byzantine, so the inclusion of s is preferred. In conclusion, both internal and external evidence favor the reading "upon earth peace to men with whom God is pleased."

In 1 John 3:1, following "Behold what sort of love the Father has given us, that we should be called children of God," some manuscripts add the words "and we are." Could this be a case of a heretical scribe deliberately omitting this phrase to eliminate the strong assertion that we are not only *called* children of God but truly *are* his children? If so, it is heresy perpetuated by the Textus Receptus and the King James

Version! We can safely say that it is *not* an intentional heretical omission, however, because the manuscripts that omit "and we are" here agree with all other manuscripts in reading "Beloved, now we are children of God" in the very next verse. On the other hand, if the author did not originally include this phrase, a well-meaning scribe could have added it to strengthen the passage, wanting to make it clear that we truly *are* God's children.

There is another possibility, however: it might have been an unintentional error. In Greek uncial letters, the phrase "and we are" closely resembles the letters immediately preceding them in this verse; it consists of the last seven letters of the following sequence: ΚΛΗΘΩΜΕΝΚΑΙΕΣΜΕΝ. A scribe's eye could easily have skipped from the first ΜΕΝ to the second, causing him to omit the last seven letters. It thus appears that "and we are" could have been either added intentionally or omitted unintentionally.

Manuscript evidence is overwhelmingly in favor of the inclusion of the phrase. The Alexandrian and Western texts include it; only the Byzantine text, which more often adds words than omits them, nevertheless omits these words. Combining this strong external evidence with the internal evidence, we confidently conclude that John originally included the phrase "and we are" and that subsequent scribes accidentally omitted it.

Another interesting variant occurs in 1 John 4:20, of which the readings are "he is not able to love God whom he has not seen" and "how is he able to love God whom he has not seen?" An accidental error is quite unlikely in this case even though the difference in the Greek text is a matter of only two words of two and three letters respectively. As for intentional change, a scribe might have felt that "he is not able" was too absolute and softened it to "how is he able." It is also possible, but less likely, that a scribe might have intentionally changed "how is he able" to the stronger "he is not able."

In manuscript evidence, "he is not able" is Alexandrian, while "how is he able" is Byzantine and possibly Western. Considering this evidence and the probable preference of internal evidence, we conclude that the original text is "he is not able" and that a scribe weakened it to "how is he able" not from a heretical motive but from a feeling that it might not be totally impossible for a person to love God even if he did not love his brother.

In Matthew 6:1 the Alexandrian and Western texts read "Take heed to your righteousness," while the Caesarean and Byzantine texts read "alms" instead of "righteousness." The external evidence thus favors "righteousness," which we understand as referring to various acts of righteousness such as those Jesus goes on to mention: alms (v. 2), prayer (v. 5), and fasting (v. 16). If "alms" was original, it would hardly have been changed by a scribe to the much less obvious "righteousness." It is much more likely that a scribe thought that "righteousness" in verse 1 meant the same thing as "alms" in verse 2, so he changed the more general word to the more specific word for the sake of clarity. Both internal and external evidence, then, support "righteousness" as the original text here.

In Matthew 6:4, after the phrase "your father who sees in the secret place will reward you" the Byzantine text adds the word "openly," but the other three text-types omit this word. External evidence thus favors the omission. As for internal evidence, there is no apparent reason for "openly" to have been omitted either accidentally or intentionally if it was original. If it was not original, however, it would have been very easy for a scribe to add it to make a more complete contrast with the word "secretly" in the preceding clause. Both lines of evidence thus favor the omission of "openly." Jesus was making the point that God will reward righteous deeds, not necessarily that the reward will be obvious to everyone. Incidentally, the same variant occurs in verse 18 with even less manuscript support.

Some Important Variants

Let us now look at some more significant variants, instances in which the meaning of the passage is affected to some extent by the readings.

In Mark 1:1 most manuscripts read "The beginning of

the gospel of Jesus Christ, Son of God," but some manuscripts omit "Son of God." Heresy! someone cries. But let's take a closer look. First, from internal evidence we see that if Mark did not include the phrase "Son of God" here, a pious scribe could easily have added it. But if the phrase was part of the original text, would a heretical scribe have omitted it? If he did so, why would this presumed heretic leave the word "Christ," which is an exalted title for Jesus, in the text? Furthermore, the very manuscripts that omit "Son of God" here include these very words in Mark 15:40, in which the Roman centurion, seeing Jesus die, calls him "Son of God."

It is more likely that the phrase is original and was omitted accidentally. The last three letters of the word "gospel" plus the phrase "Jesus Christ Son of God" would have been written as IOYῙΥΧΥΥΥΘΥ in an early Greek manuscript. The repetition of the letter Y could have caused a scribe's eye to skip over the last four letters, which form the regular Greek abbreviation for "Son of God." Turning to external evidence, we find that only Codex Aleph of the Alexandrian text and part of the Caesarean text omit "Son of God" here, while almost all of the Alexandrian, part of the Caesarean, and the Western and Byzantine texts include the phrase. Manuscript evidence therefore strongly supports the inclusion of the phrase. Since internal evidence indicates that the phrase was probably omitted accidentally, we conclude from both lines of evidence that "Son of God" was part of the original text of Mark 1:1.

A significant variant is found in Acts 8:37. After the Ethiopian official asks Philip "What hinders me from being baptized?" some manuscripts add verse 37, as follows: "And Philip said, 'If you believe with all your heart, you can be.' And he answered and said, 'I believe that Jesus Christ is the Son of God.' " Other manuscripts omit this dialogue and immediately after the Ethiopian's question continue with verse 38: "And he commanded the chariot to stop. . . ."

Verse 37 could hardly have been either added or omitted accidentally. Moreover, it is highly unlikely that the verse was intentionally omitted by a heretic wanting to eliminate this confession concerning Jesus Christ, because the same manuscripts that omit this verse include acknowledgments of Jesus as the Son of God a few verses later, in 9:20. On the other hand, if the author of Acts did not provide the exchange recorded in this verse, it would have been tempting for a scribe to do so, since the question in verse 36 must have received a reply.

The manuscript support for verse 37 is very weak, consisting only of part of the Western text. The verse is not found even in the Byzantine text. Although the verse appears in the Textus Receptus and therefore in the King James Version, it was not in the manuscript Erasmus used principally for Acts in his first published Greek New Testament in 1516. He found this passage as a marginal addition to another manuscript of Acts and added it in a later edition, thinking that it must have been original but that it had been omitted from his other manuscript by accident.

The Ethiopian official surely must have confessed his faith in Jesus before Philip baptized him, either before or after he raised the question of baptism. That Philip's question and the official's confession were not part of the original text here, however, is certain on the basis of both internal and external evidence. Incidentally, if someone wonders why this addition has a verse number if it was not original, he should remember that our verse numbers were not put into the text until the fourth edition of Stephanus in 1551, as we noted earlier—long after Erasmus had included the verse.

In Mark 9:29 Jesus says of the unclean spirit he had expelled from a boy, "This kind cannot be driven out except by prayer," or as other manuscripts read, "by prayer and fasting." The words "and fasting" could hardly have been either added or omitted accidentally. Neither is it likely that the phrase was omitted intentionally in prejudice against fasting, because the same manuscripts that omit "and fasting" here include a favorable reference to fasting in Mark 2:18-20. However, if Mark did not originally include this phrase, an early scribe could easily have added it to emphasize the spiritual effort involved in the exorcism. Internal evidence, then, favors the omission of "and fasting" here.

Most manuscripts include "and fasting," however. Only

the two best Alexandrian manuscripts (Codd. Aleph and B), one Western witness, one Caesarean witness, and one Church Father's quotation omit it. External evidence, then, is doubtful but may favor the addition. However, if a scribe added these words in a manuscript, the increasing emphasis in the early church on the necessity of fasting might have attracted other scribes to the addition even if they knew that it was not found in all manuscripts in their day. Internal evidence, therefore, leads to the conclusion that "and fasting" was not an original part of Mark here, even though fasting is favorably mentioned elsewhere.

It is worth noting that the phrase "and fasting" is added by some manuscripts in 1 Corinthians 7:5 as well, following the words "that you may devote yourselves to prayer." Here, however, the manuscript support for the addition is only Byzantine, and it is clearly not original.

Protestants conclude the Lord's Prayer with the doxology "For thine is the kingdom and the power and the glory forever. Amen." This version of the doxology appears in Matthew 6:13 in the Byzantine text, part of the Caesarean, and some Alexandrian witnesses, while the Western text, part of the Alexandrian, and part of the Caesarean omit it. Manuscript evidence therefore favors the omission, although not strongly.

The doxology is omitted by all witnesses from the Lord's Prayer recorded in Luke 11:2-4. It is not likely that the doxology would have been omitted either accidentally or intentionally from Matthew if it had been original. However, since without it the prayer seems to end a bit abruptly, when it came to be used in worship services a doxology such as this could easily have been added. From this use it could have been added to the manuscripts by scribes who thought that its use in worship indicated that it must have been as much a part of the original text as the prayer itself. The conclusion, then, strongly from internal evidence and to a lesser degree from external evidence, is that the doxology was not part of the original text of Matthew. Of course, it is still perfectly proper to use the doxology when repeating the prayer in worship or devotions. It should be remembered that when Jesus gave this prayer to his disciples he was not giving them a liturgical form to repeat but rather was teaching them how simply and directly they could talk to their heavenly father.

In 1 Corinthians 6:20 the question is whether Paul simply says "Therefore glorify God in your body" or whether he adds "and in your spirit, which are God's." The added words are a perfectly proper exhortation, but if they were original, there is no reasonable way to account for their having been omitted in so many good manuscripts. On the other hand, if they were not original, a devout scribe could have added them, possibly in an effort to guard against the idea that we should glorify God only with our physical bodies. We should, of course, glorify God with our spirits as well, but in this passage (1 Cor. 6:12-20) the Apostle is speaking specifically of the physical body, and the reference to the human spirit here is not in harmony with the context.

The omission of the reference to the spirit is strongly supported by the Alexandrian and Western text-types, while the addition is supported by the Byzantine. Both internal and external evidence, therefore, make it clear that Paul's words here are simply "Therefore glorify God in your body" as an emphatic summary of his discussion of the sanctity of our bodies.

Three Longer Variants

There is a textual variant in John 5:3-4 that we should examine. Following the reference to the sick people at the Pool of Bethesda in verse 3, some manuscripts add that they were "waiting for the moving of the water; [4] for an angel of the Lord went down at certain seasons into the pool and troubled the water; whoever stepped in first after the troubling of the water was healed of whatever disease he had." Other manuscripts omit this final part of verse 3 and all of verse 4.

That these words were original and were omitted accidentally is very unlikely, since none of the elements that commonly lead to accidental omission are present. Furthermore, an ancient scribe would have had no reason to omit this reference intentionally, since it gives relevant information. Nor would the reference to an angel's activity have been a problem for a scribe; the manuscripts that omit this passage freely include references to angels in other parts of the Gospels. On the other hand, if John did not originally include this explanation of the popular belief in the curative power of the pool, it would have been a very natural thing for an early copyist who knew of the tradition to add it. Indeed, a scribe might have put these words in the margin of his manuscript not intending to add them to the text of the Gospel but simply giving a note to explain what happened at the pool. A later scribe, seeing the note in the margin of the manuscript as he was copying from it, might then have taken it to be a part of the Gospel text that had been accidentally omitted and later added in the margin (which was done at times) and on that basis have incorporated it into his manuscript. The addition would then have been included in all further copies made from this manuscript.

Additional evidence against the likelihood that this passage was in the original manuscript is the fact that six or seven words or phrases in it are not used anywhere else in John's Gospel; indeed, three of the words are found nowhere else in the New Testament.

As for manuscript evidence, the passage is omitted in the best part of the Alexandrian text, including two of the oldest papyrus manuscripts (P⁶⁶ and P⁷⁵) as well as part of the Western text. It is included by the Caesarean and Byzantine and by some witnesses of the other two text-types. Many manuscripts that include the passage have notations indicating that it was not considered to be a part of the original text. Both the internal and the strong external evidence make it clear that this explanatory note was not part of John's text but was added later.

There are two significant passages in the New Testament in which a textual variant involves several verses. One of these is John 7:53–8:11, the story of the woman taken in adultery. The question here is not whether the story is true—as John 20:30 reminds us, Jesus did many things that are not recorded in the Gospels—but simply whether John included this story when he wrote his Gospel.

Let us look at the external evidence first. We would not question the passage if it were present in all of the manuscripts, but it is omitted by the Alexandrian text—including Codices Aleph and B and two of the oldest papyri (P[66] and P[75])—as well as by part of the Caesarean and Western texts and by a variety of versions and Church Fathers. Other manuscripts include the passage here but with notations indicating doubt that it is genuine. Still other manuscripts place the story after Luke 21:38, after John 7:36, at the very end of Luke, or at the very end of John. Furthermore, the story is not commented on by any Greek Church Father until the twelfth century, and the first Greek Father who does so states that accurate copies of the Gospel do not contain the passage. In view of the vast extent of ancient commentaries on the New Testament, it would be incredible that they would not have dealt with a story such as this if the Church Fathers had considered it a genuine part of John's Gospel.

Among witnesses that include this passage at this point with no indication of doubt concerning it are part of the Western text, the Byzantine text, and some other manuscripts and Latin Church Fathers that are not classified under the recognized text-types. The manuscript evidence, then, is decisively against considering this passage as an original part of John's Gospel.

Turning to internal evidence, the passage is obviously too long to have been omitted accidentally from more than one or two manuscripts. But could it have been omitted intentionally by scribes who felt that the story dealt too leniently with a sin as serious as adultery? This seems unlikely, inasmuch as there is no indication that any scribes attempted to delete either the story in Luke 7:36-50 of the gentle treatment that Jesus gave to the "sinful woman" who anointed his feet or the statement in Luke 23:43 of Jesus' promise of forgiveness to the repentant thief on the cross. Furthermore, if a scribe had wished to delete this story, there would have been no necessity for him to eliminate 7:53–8:2, which would have joined well with 8:12.

It is especially significant to observe that this passage contains many Greek words and forms of words that are not in harmony with the style or vocabulary of the rest of the Gospel. Indeed, one scholar pointed out a number of years ago that the passage more closely resembles the vocabulary and style of Luke than of John. In the final analysis, then, although this story may very well be true, since it is not inconsistent with other Gospel accounts about Jesus, it is nevertheless clear that it cannot be called a part of the inspired gospel record.

The second of these major textual problems involves the ending of Mark. The Alexandrian Codices Sinaiticus and Vaticanus (Aleph and B) both omit Mark 16:9-20, as does the second-century Church Father Cyril of Alexandria and a few other witnesses. In addition, the Ammonian Sections (a system of section divisions for each of the Gospels developed in the early fourth century that is something like our verse divisions but generally longer) stop at Mark 16:8. Two third-century Church Fathers who quote Scripture very extensively make no reference to these closing verses in their writings. Among the manuscripts that do contain these verses, some have notations indicating that there is doubt that they are part of the original text, while others insert the following brief passage before verse 9 to smooth the otherwise rough transition between verses 8 and 9: "for they were afraid. But they reported briefly to Peter and those who were with him all that they had been told. And after this Jesus himself sent out through them, from east to west, the sacred and imperishable proclamation of eternal salvation. Now when he had arisen...." In addition, one fifth-century manuscript also includes a ninety-word addition following verse 14.

Although the great majority of the manuscripts and versions do contain verses 9-20, the evidence for the omission of these verses is too strong to be passed over. Let us consider the factors involved.

If the Greek text of 16:9-20 harmonized with the rest of the Gospel, we would be inclined to suppose that these verses had been accidentally omitted from the witnesses mentioned above. For one thing, if the verses are omitted the Gospel is left with no record of the appearances of Jesus after his resurrection. Indeed, the Gospel without these verses ends on a note of pessimism and frustration: "And they went out and fled from the tomb, for trembling and astonishment had seized them; and they said nothing to anyone, for they were afraid." More than this, the final word in the Greek text is the conjunction "for" (the Greek "for" cannot stand first in a clause, so it follows the Greek verb here), which is simply not the sort of construction any author would normally create.

The problem, however, is not so simple. The words and forms in these verses are so different from the rest of the Gospel that a student who had read Mark in Greek up to this point but had not read any of the rest of the New Testament in Greek would find himself in unfamiliar material in these last verses. Furthermore, as we have noted, the connection between verses 8 and 9 is exceedingly harsh. The subject changes from "the women" in verse 8 to "Jesus" in verse 9, and yet Jesus is not named. In verse 9 the writer tells us who Mary Magdalene is, although she has already been named in verse 1. There is another small but significant point. In the seven other instances in the New Testament in which the phrase "the first day of the week" occurs, including one instance in Mark 16:2, the Greek form is literally "day one" rather than "the first day." Yet in Mark 16:9 the form is "the first day"—which sounds better in English but is not the characteristic New Testament form.

If, then, verses 9-20 are not an original part of the Gospel, what do we make of the situation? The most reasonable answer is that the original ending of Mark was lost at a very early date and that a scribe wrote verses 9-20 in an attempt to supply a suitable ending for the Gospel.

How might the final part of the Gospel have been lost? Early in this book we noted that the original manuscripts—the autographs—of the Gospels were written on papyrus, likely in scroll form. When someone finished reading a scroll, the outer part of the scroll would be the end of the book if the reader did not bother to reroll it. It is possible that the autograph of Mark, or a very early copy, could have been left without being rerolled, in which case the last one or two spirals of the scroll could have been accidentally torn off. On the other hand, we also noted that at a very early date manuscripts of the New Testament were also produced in codex form, like our present books; it is possible that even the original or at least one of the earliest copies was produced in this form. If this were the case, it would have been even easier for the final quire or the final one or two sheets to have been torn off accidentally, leaving the Gospel with the abrupt ending at 16:8.

In summary, then, it is unbelievable that the author closed his Gospel at 16:8. But still, internal evidence, supported by a reasonable amount of external evidence, strongly indicates that verses 9-20 as we know them were not part of the original manuscript and therefore cannot be called inspired scripture. The only fair conclusion seems to be that the ending of Mark was lost very soon after it was written and that verses 9-20 are the result of a scribe's attempt to supply an acceptable ending.

CHAPTER NINE

What Shall We Say to These Things?

What conclusions can we draw from all that we have said? How should we look upon the text of the New Testament as it is reflected in the Greek text available to us today as well as in the common English versions that are being read?

In these pages we have seen that the great majority of textual differences between the manuscripts are matters of small details that have no real theological significance. To underscore this fact, I would cite the following list of variants in addition to those we have already looked at:

Philippians 1:14—"to speak the word" / "to speak the word of God"

1 Thessalonians 2:15—"who killed both the Lord Jesus and the prophets" / "who killed both the Lord Jesus and their own prophets"

2 Timothy 2:14—"before God" / "before the Lord"

Titus 1:10—"many who are insubordinate" / "many who are also insubordinate"

2 Thessalonians 2:8—"whom the Lord will destroy" / "whom the Lord Jesus will destroy"

John 5:17—"but he [the context obviously indicating Jesus] answered them" / "but Jesus answered them"

Acts 2:24—""the pains of death" / "the pains of Hades"

Mark 8:26—"Don't even go into the village" / "Don't tell it to anyone in the village" / "Don't even go into the village nor tell it to anyone in the village" / "Go into your house and don't tell it to anyone in the village" / "Go into your house and if you go into the village don't tell it to anyone, not even in the village" / "Go into your house and if you go into the village don't tell it to anyone" / "Go into your house and don't even go into the village nor tell it to anyone in the village" / "And if you go into the village don't tell it to anyone in the village"

The list could be extended for longer than anyone would care to read. I present it for a specific reason. There are those who insist that some of the manuscripts most scholars consider reliable have in fact been intentionally corrupted to omit or weaken important doctrines of the Christian faith. I offer three points in rebuttal of this claim:

1. As we have just noted, by far the most variants have no theological significance at all. If some scribes were intent on corrupting the text of the New Testament, why would they devote most of their efforts to producing changes in their manuscripts that did not in fact corrupt it?

2. It cannot be demonstrated that any of the Greek manuscripts of the New Testament we recognize to be valid in any way consistently weakens, perverts, or omits any theological point or doctrine. On the contrary, manuscripts that critics condemn for omitting or changing a supposedly significant word or phrase in one passage will invariably be seen to contain the same word or idea in other passages. If the variant indicates an attempt to corrupt the text, why did the scribe content himself with corrupting it in one passage but not in other passages?

3. It is not without significance that the very manuscripts or texts that these critics acclaim as the true and faithful texts are occasionally guilty of the very type of variant they call heresy in other texts. For example, it is the Byzantine text-type and the Textus Receptus that in 1 John 3:1 omit the strong words "and we are [children of God]." Just a few verses earlier, in 1 John 2:23, it is again the Byzantine text and the Textus Receptus that omit the entire clause "he who

confesses the Son has the Father also." Such omissions are precisely the sort of thing such critics are inclined to decry as heresy elsewhere.

The truth, of course, is that such charges of deliberate corruption are false. Let us remind ourselves again that scribes were engaged in copying the text, not in studying it, when they did their work. Indeed, many textual errors arose from the very fact that the scribe was not thinking of the meaning or the full sense of the passage he was copying.

To get an idea of the sort of arguments that are sometimes used, it may be worth referring to some notes I received from a message given by a well-known clergyman from Northern Ireland. In this message he attacked the New International Version of the New Testament specifically, but his charges were actually directed against the Greek text from which this English version was translated, which is essentially the text I have been supporting in this book and which most recent versions follow. Among his comments were the following:

Matthew 1:25—Because the NIV follows the Greek reading "until she gave birth to a son" instead of the King James Version's "till she had brought forth her first-born son," this clergyman charged the NIV with "striking at the virgin birth of Christ"! In actual fact, of course, the variant has nothing whatever to do with the question of the virgin birth, and the criticism is sheer rabble-rousing. Indeed, since this particular clergyman is violently anti–Roman Catholic, he could more logically (but still fallaciously) have seen the NIV reading as an accommodation to the Roman Catholic doctrine that Mary had no more children after the birth of Jesus!

Luke 2:33—Because the NIV reads "the child's father and mother marveled" where the KJV reads "Joseph and his mother marvelled," this clergyman charges that the NIV implies that Joseph was the father of Jesus, thus denying the virgin birth. He conveniently overlooks Luke 2:48, only a few lines farther on, in which the KJV and all other versions quote Mary herself as saying to Jesus that *"your father and I* have been anxiously searching for you"!

Matthew 25:13—He charges that by reading "Therefore

keep watch, because you do not know the day or the hour"
and omitting the addition found in the KJV, "wherein the Son
of man cometh," the NIV is "striking at the second coming
of Christ." This is patently a false accusation. This sort of
reference to the "day" and the "hour" clearly implies the return of Christ. More than this, the whole context from the
beginning of chapter 24 bespeaks the second coming of Christ.

Charges such as these must be ascribed to ignorance,
willful prejudice, or both.

Differences Other Than Variants

It is important to remember that not all differences mentioned in our common English versions arise from differences
between ancient manuscripts; many result from different
interpretations of the same Greek word or phrase into English. To signal these different possibilities, both the RSV and
the NIV include footnotes consisting of the word *Or* followed
by the alternate interpretation. For example, in John 2:23 the
NIV text reads "believed in his name," and the footnote reads
"Or *and believed in him.*" In John 3:3 the text of the Revised
Standard Version reads "anew," and the footnote reads "Or
from above." If the difference is a textual variant, on the other
hand, the footnote will state "Other ancient authorities read,"
"Some early MSS read," or something similar. For example,
in Luke 22:16 the RSV text reads "not eat it," and the footnote reads, "Other ancient authorities read *never eat it again.*"

And Finally . . .

What can we conclude from our study of the manuscripts
of the New Testament as they were copied and handed down
through these nearly two thousand years?

We see that the inspired New Testament text was a Greek
text and that any translation can be considered to be the Word
of God only insofar as it presents the message that was given
by the original authors in Greek. Only they, and no later
scribes, editors, or translators, were given the unique inspi-

ration of the Holy Spirit to put God's revelation into human words.

We see that in the thousands of manuscripts of the New Testament that were copied through the centuries and the millions of words they contain there are countless differences of words, word order, and word forms. Yet the evidence is clear that most of these differences are accidental or insignificant and that when scribes intentionally changed a text they usually did so to clarify or strengthen the meaning; there is virtually no evidence of a scribe intentionally trying to weaken or corrupt the text. We have seen, in addition, that by use of established and reasonable principles we can decide between variants in most instances and determine which is the original reading.

Finally, and very importantly, we see that we do not have to close our minds to the history of the New Testament text in order to prevent our confidence in the New Testament as we have it from being weakened or destroyed. Rather, we can be certain that God has preserved his Word down through the centuries. Sir Frederic Kenyon, one of the greatest and most respected scholars of New Testament manuscripts of the past century, expresses this conviction well when he closes his book *The Story of the Bible* with these words: "It is reassuring at the end to find that the general result of all these discoveries and all this study is to strengthen the proof of the authenticity of the Scriptures, and our conviction that we have in our hands, in substantial integrity, the veritable Word of God."

Subject-Name Index

Scripture Reference Index

Passages appearing in boldface type are discussed in the text, briefly or in detail.